GSMD

A Hundred Years' Per

Hugh Barty-King

GSMD

A

HUNDRED YEARS'

PERFORMANCE

Published for the Guildhall School of Music and Drama
Barbican, London, EC2Y 8DT

by

Stainer & Bell Ltd, 82 High Road, London N2 9PW

ISBN: 0 85249 589 7

Printed in Great Britain by Galliard (Printers) Ltd, Great Yarmouth

Contents

Prelude

Maurice Hart

This book chronicles the history of the Guildhall School of Music and Drama for the first time. It refers frequently to the Music Committee of the Corporation of the City of London, of which I have the honour to be its present Chairman.

The rôle of the Committee seems to puzzle even those closely involved with the School. Among the students, curious myths have grown up. The acting students seem to think that the Committee is the censorship body that decides which plays the drama department is allowed to put on! There is absolutely no truth in that rumour, I hasten to add. The professors think that the Music Committee controls the Corporation's money bags. There is no truth in that either. The Committee is responsible for monitoring the finances of the School, but decisions about the level of expenditure are made by other Corporation Committees, and by the Court of Common Council itself. Nevertheless, as the Committee responsible for the School, the Music Committee must be completely familiar with the artistic and educational policies of the School, in order to present its case to the rest of the Corporation. The School is run by specialists drawn from the world of music and drama, but rarely can the Music Committee count either musicians or educationalists amongst its members. The Committee is made up of professional City men and women concerned and interested in the School. The combination of the interested layman from the City and the specialist staff from the School makes for a fruitful fusion of complementary talents. The natural caution of the business man is often needed to underpin the volatile schemes of the artist. The working relationship between the School and the Committee has been, by and large, extremely successful throughout the last hundred years.

Perhaps the most crucial function of the Music Committee has been the selection of the Principal, because it is largely the Principal who initiates policy and gives the School its sense of direction. The history of the School suggests that the collective wisdom of lay people has worked to the advantage of the School. Certainly it seems to have chosen the appropriate Principal for the appropriate stage in the development of the School. Each one has come in with a set of objectives over and above keeping the School running as it was. The chapter headings give an indication of what concerned each Principal, and what he achieved.

However, a general policy for the School was declared by Sir Landon Ronald in 1910: it would be 'absolutely modern and progressive'. To be modern means to equip the young performer with the skills needed today in a profession which calls for a combination of nerve, skill and innate artistry that only the best training will allow to develop.

It is interesting to discover that the Guildhall School of Music and Drama exists only because of the imagination, initiative and persuasiveness not of a musician, but of a member of the Court of Common Council, John Bath whose brainchild the Corporation School of Music at Aldermanbury was, and who was Chairman eighty Chairmen before me.

A centenary always provides an opportunity for self-indulgence. Looking back over its hundred years of existence, those of us who have been closely associated with the 'GSMD' will feel a great deal of pride in its achievements. However we should also develop a sense of proportion and perspective about its problems. The cost of the School to City's Cash seems always to have got to crisis point, there have always been extreme accommodation difficulties that have been miraculously but temporarily resolved. History never teaches us how to avoid problems or making mistakes. The lesson we learn from history is that there have always been the same problems and we have always made the same mistakes. As one battles through a new recession, through new disasters both national and international, I suppose it is of some comfort to know that every generation has been through its own crises. When we face yet another 'period of transition' it is worth reflecting that Adam may well have said to Eve, as they left the Garden of Eden, "We live, my dear, in an age of transition"....

But we must not look only at the past: the journey between the Warehouse at Aldermanbury and the sophisticated new Barbican

School has been momentous. But ahead lies the opening of the Arts and Conference Centre at the Barbican, housing some of the greatest performing talents in the world. The School cannot but gain enormously by having such neighbours. Certainly the Barbican will become a major cultural and artistic powerhouse in Europe; certainly it demonstrates the City's commitment to the Arts which has always been traditionally manifested through its own music and drama school, the 'GSMD'.

PART ONE

'It is only within the last twenty or thirty years that Art of all kinds has become a matter of general public interest, and amongst the Arts it was natural that Music should come into the front rank in public estimation. But in these early days few would have been sufficiently sanguine to foretell that within a quarter of a century a music-school would arise, supported by the funds and fostered by the care of the Corporation of the City of London, which was destined to become the largest institution of the kind in the world!

Many now living will remember the poor opinion generally held by the average English parent as to the advantage of music in education of their children. It was conceded that it might be a good thing for young girls to learn to strum on the piano, or warble a ballad of a common-place type; but for men and women it was unworthy of serious attention. How far this prejudice against music, as being an effeminate study, was dissipated by the results of the Franco-German war, in which the most musical nation in the world proved itself to be the most muscular and war-like, may be doubtful; but one thing is certain, that from that time we have heard no more of fathers threatening to cut their sons off with the proverbial shilling if they found them displaying any serious interest in the despised art.

Instead of this we find the Art of Music taken up and adopted by the highest classes (thanks to the initiative of our Royal Family) and soon becoming the fashion; having got its chance, it was clear that a study so full of charm, and possessing such possibilities as a social force, should not remain subject to the fluctuations of fashion. It was inevitable that it should work its way into the hearts of a naturally music-loving people, and be adopted and cherished as a permanent and valued thing.'

Sir Joseph Barnby, Principal, Guildhall School of Music
The Strand Musical Magazine, March 1895

The old Warehouse in Aldermanbury, used as the first
School Premises, 1880–1886

1 The City Waits—On The Prince of Wales

'It was just a glorious show,' scoffed Byron's friend John Cam Hobhouse in scornful dismissal of Prince Albert's brainchild the Great Exhibition of 1851. 'It did not bring international peace, it did not improve taste. Imperceptibly it might have promoted free trade; a few manufacturers might have learned from their foreign rivals. That is all, bar an empty building and a large financial surplus.'

But it was under the influence of the way in which royalty insisted that some of this surplus should be applied, that Victorian bankers and merchants who had seen no reason for allowing Music to interfere with the all-consuming, manly pursuit of wealth, allowed themselves to be converted to the view of those who gave the role of the City a wider interpretation and deplored the departure of Minstrelsy.

The City's first academy had stemmed from the charter which King Edward IV had granted in 1469. His guild of 13 minstrels was governed by a marshal and two wardens who examined the pretensions of all who assumed to exercise the minstrel profession, and supplied the City's musical watchmen—the wachts or waits. A century later Sir Thomas Gresham, in a will dated 5 July 1575, directed that after the death of his wife his house in Bishopsgate Street should be converted into a college in which lectures should be given on a number of subjects including Music. In 1663 Charles II turned it into the Royal Society of London. Following a revision of Gresham's will which set up various trusts through the Mercers Company, the Corporation of London undertook to pay £50 a year to each of the seven professors giving the Gresham Lectures, one of which was still Music. The house in Bishopsgate Street which had become Gresham College was then bequeathed to the Corporation. It was demolished in 1768 to make room for the new Excise Office, and in 1842 the Corporation built a new college with a fine theatre/concert hall at the corner of Gresham Street and Basinghall Street, the site which the rebuilt college of 1913 still occupies. The Corporation and the Mercers Company jointly control the Gresham Estate and carry out the will through a Joint Grand Gresham Committee.

A body calling itself the Royal Academy of Music had been formed in 1720, but this consisted of noblemen and gentlemen who gave large sums and received subscriptions merely for the establishment in London of Italian Opera. However, the £50,000 which they raised was soon lost in wrangling over which works should be performed, and the society with the pretentious title was forgotten.

In 1728 Daniel Defoe had put forward a detailed scheme for a Music School as part of the Christ's Hospital School in Newgate Street, but his imaginative scheme for a City equivalent of Vivaldi's Ospedale in Venice came to nothing.

A more worthy and lasting bearer of the name 'Royal Academy of Music' was formed with a royal charter in 1822, 'to promote the cultivation of the science of Music and afford facilities for attaining perfection in it by assisting with general instruction the natives of this country . . . and provide for themselves the means of an honourable and comfortable livelihood'—for would-be professionals in other words.

It was the idea of John Fane, Lord Burghersh, who for some time was British Ambassador in Florence. On the death of his father, he succeeded to the title of Earl of Westmorland. His academy provided teaching and residence for ten girls and ten boys between the ages of 10 and 14 in the empty West End town house of the Earl of Carnarvon off Hanover Square. The inaugural 20 pupils were personally selected by King George IV. 'The first object in the education of the students will consist in a strict attention to their religious and moral instruction.' Dr William Crotch was first Principal.

Nine years later there appeared within the City at Milton Street, Cripplegate a 'School of Practical Instruction for Elocution, Music and Drama' opened by one John Kemble Chapman in what had been the City Chapel. He announced that the City Pantheon, as he called it, 'is intended to comprise a systematic course of Tuition in Elocution, Acting, Dramatic Reading, Vocal Music, Dancing, Fencing & C; and to afford students and amateurs frequent opportunities of respectable practice; and foster and develop talents which without such advantages might be entirely lost to their possessors and the public.'

Representation of the house as a School of Music and Drama was in fact a ploy by Chapman to outwit those who would enforce the Act of Parliament which forbade dramatic shows except in a licensed Patent Theatre which the City Theatre he opened in Cripplegate in 1831 certainly was not. Though continually harassed by the patentees, Chapman managed to survive for quite a long time— mounting Shakespeare by companies which included Edmund Kean and Ellen Terry at the outset of their careers—but it never offered any real competition to the aristocratically sponsored academy in the West End.

In 1854 Lord Westmorland and his Governing Committee applied to the Commissioners for the Great Exhibition of 1851 for a site on which to build a new Royal Academy of Music, but were refused. On his lordship's death in 1859 the personal backing which had enabled the academy to survive was withdrawn, and the Committee appealed to the Government for help. But the Lords of the Treasury were not prepared to subsidise a seemingly lame duck of a music school on an annual basis, and authorised payment of a single grant of £500 to relieve its immediate embarrassment. When William Sterndale Bennett became Principal in 1866 the Royal Academy of Music was on the verge of bankruptcy; and when it celebrated its golden jubilee in 1872 it was urged by the Society of Arts to move to rooms in the new Albert Hall which had been completed the previous year. Sensing a threat to its independence, the Governing Committee refused to do anything of the sort, announced their intention of re-modelling its Tenterden Street premises and opened a Building Fund.

It was well known that it had been the Prince Consort's cherished wish to create a national training school for music; and had he not died so unexpectedly in 1861 there is no doubt that he would have personally steered some of the 'large financial surplus' earned by his Hyde Park Exhibition towards the realisation of just such a project. As C. R. Fay pointed out in his centenary publication *Palace of Industry 1851*, the Prince Consort had an intellectual urge to applied science, 'but his heart was in music and the arts, and in the greatness of his adopted country.' And in that country in the eighteen-seventies the performance and writing of music by its 'natives' had sunk to its nadir. Ten years after Albert's death, his son Edward, the Prince of Wales, who was well aware of his father's idealistic ambitions, thought the time had come to do something about raising it.

Since a Royal Academy of Music was already in existence, of which his great-grandfather had been patron, it seemed obvious to the Prince that that ailing institution should be given new life as the nucleus of the National Training School for Music which his father had in mind. He was not alone in this view. It was the 'settled conviction' of the Commissioners for the Great Exhibition 'that the union of the Royal Academy of Music and the National Training School would have been the best means of promoting the national development of high musical training.' They heard with satisfaction, they declared, that an important movement under the leadership of the Prince of Wales and Prince Christian of Denmark had been made to establish a National College of Music 'on a more permanent and wider basis than any other institution, and the union of the Royal Academy of Music and the National Training School for Music formed a central object of that movement.' But once again the Governing Committee of the RAM set their face against any move which might lead to an alteration in their royal constitution and the benefits it bestowed. So the RAM was by-passed, and in 1873 the Commissioners granted a site for the new Training School near the Albert Hall in Kensington Gore at a rental of £80 a year. The foundation stone was laid by HRH the Duke of Edinburgh on 13 December 1873.

In 1872 Rev H. G. Bonavia Hunt had founded the Church Choral Society and College of Church Music whose first meetings were held in the schoolroom of St Botolphs, Bishopsgate. In 1875 it had been incorporated under the title Trinity College, London, with Academical and Choral divisions. The following year it leased 61 Weymouth Street, Marylebone. The renowned tenor Sims Reeves was a singing teacher and Sir Joseph Barnby was among the examiners. On 1 June 1880 Trinity College of Music moved to 13 Mandeville Place, Marylebone.

The thought of the West End having three conservatoires stirred the musical conscience of the City fathers as nothing else had done. Matthew Arnold had just asserted that the people who believed most that Britain's greatness and welfare 'are proved by our being very rich ... are just the very people whom we call the Philistines'. The Corporation had no wish to justify an accusation of Philistinism, and when the Lord Mayor received an invitation from Buckingham Palace he gladly sent a deputation to wait on the Prince of Wales to discuss the possibility of the City providing money for musical scholarships to the National Training School. The Corporation's offer to found ten free scholarships of £40 each for five years in the West End establishment was gratefully accepted: the City had become a founding patron of the future Royal College of Music.

Subsidising the Kensington Gore operation was a gesture designed to show the Men of Music that the Men of Business were ready to maintain something other than what Charles Lamb described as the Pulse of Gain. But there were members of the Corporation who wanted to go even further. One of them was the member for the Bridge Ward, John Bath, who on 17 September 1873, three months before the royal duke laid the foundation stone of the National Training School (which opened on 17 May 1876), moved a reference from the Court of Common Council 'as to the best means of providing approved musical performances & c in the Guildhall, or in any other way to patronise the science of music in the City of London and for the public benefit.' He proposed that the Court of Common Council should patronise the organisation of a Free Orchestral and Vocal Association to be called the Musical Society of the City of London, and bear its annual expense. It would consist of 500 to 1,000 people 'to be educated from week to week in the noblest of all the sciences.' The cost of such a Musical Society he estimated at £200 a year, but he was sure that the best amateur musicians who worked during the day in the City would make their contribution. The way for a society on these lines had been prepared by the Musical Lecture which the Corporation had already founded at Gresham College.

John Bath was ahead of his time. The minds of the Common Councillors of 1873 were not attuned to the favourable acceptance of so far-reaching a plan, but sounding it out at this time had made it more likely to strike a chord the second time round.

In 1875 the Corporation organised the Councillors who had made up the deputation to the Prince of Wales into a formal 'Musical Deputation' to supervise the nomination, examination and election of the ten boys and girls whose musical education at the National Training School was to be paid for out of Corporation funds. The minute of the first formal meeting of the 'Deputation Re National Training School for Music', dated 28 March 1876, records that in order to select ten they nominated 186 candidates and examined 139. But with the opportunity given them by their formal appointment as a

Committee of the Common Council, John Bath and his like-minded colleagues inevitably found themselves talking well beyond their brief, and throwing up ideas for how the Corporation could further involve itself in the World of Music.

The start point was the 300-year old institution in Basinghall Street, part-owned by the Corporation which sponsored its Musical Lectures. At their meeting of 5 July 1876, an order of reference from the Court of Common Council was read which bade them confer with the Joint Grand Gresham Committee 'upon the best means of providing for Musical Education in the Gresham College or Theatre when the same is not otherwise occupied'. On 29 September the Music Deputation duly met the Gresham Committee and discussed the possibility of using the college 'for the purpose of a school for Music'. On 25 October they considered a letter from the Mercers Company 'asking for further information in reference to the use of the Theatre of Gresham College as a School for Music'. They approved a reply in which they said they would 'probably adopt a Scheme for Musical Education which would comprise instruction in singing, Pianoforte playing and that of other instruments, and also the science of Harmony, and that they would desire to have such use of the Gresham College as would allow the Professor to attend for the purpose of giving instruction at various hours on any days, except Saturdays, which the Gresham Committee would be able to place at the Deputation's disposal'.

After due consideration the Gresham Committee turned the idea down. In a letter dated 5 December 1876 they told the Court of Common Council's Music Deputation that since Gresham College would be 'under the New Scheme [?] and fully occupied, it could not be made available for a School of Music'.

For some reason, the Music Deputation did not meet in 1877 at all. This letter was not read to them until the meeting of 20 March 1878 at which they elected John Bath their chairman. With their plans for a City School of Music based on Gresham College rejected, the Deputation concentrated on the Corporation's involvement in the National Training School for Music at Kensington Gore, whose principal was now Dr Arthur Sullivan and whose five principal professors included Dr John Stainer. It had 13 other professors including a lady teacher, Edith Jerningham. Its four professional examiners were Charles Hallé, John Hullah, Professor Ella and

Sir George Elvey. It took private pupils for not less than a year at £40 a year 'payable in advance'. Candidates for scholarships such as those given by the Corporation of London had to pass a competitive examination for which they had to be nominated by the founders of the scholarship. They could be girls or boys, and there was no age limit. They had to produce a certificate of good health, a birth certificate and a certificate signed by two well-known people in their locality that they were of good moral character. 'The object of the competitions' stated the school's prospectus, 'is to find out young persons *of any station of life* having musical talents which ought to be cultivated for the advancement of Musical Art and for the public benefit.' Scholarship candidates were also examined in reading aloud, recitation and writing from dictation, as well as the elementary principles of Music, reading and playing an instrument or singing at sight, or composition.

Blind George Macfarren had succeeded Sir William Sterndale Bennett as Principal of the Royal Academy of Music in 1875, and by 1878 it was giving tuition to some 350 pupils at its re-built Tenterden Street premises. Macfarren confirmed the stand taken by his predecessors in regard to the National Training School, and in 1878 had his directors pass a resolution that the Royal Academy of Music was willing to be placed on a more solid basis and enlarge its sphere of operation but could not surrender its charter on any conditions whatever.

The Corporation of London—or at any rate its Music Deputation— were proud to be associated with the well organised, but (for the pupils) expensive, institution at Kensington Gore supported by the leaders of the British musical world—and slightly envious. To demonstrate to aldermen and Common Council men the worth of their musical investment in the rival West End—and inculcate a desire to travel further along the same path—in September 1878 the Deputation arranged for pupils of the National Training School to give a concert in the Egyptian Hall at the Mansion House. In the following February they were followed by pupils of the RAM.

And then in the autumn of 1878 a printed letter, dated 16 November, was circulated over the signature of Charles P. Smith, late Honorary Secretary of the Brixton Amateur Musical Society, announcing that every effort was being made to establish 'a really high-class Amateur Orchestral Society to meet weekly in the City of London'. He had reason to believe that a room for practice would be gratuitously placed at the disposal of the Society. He hoped that membership would be free, but if a subscription was necessary it would not be more than a guinea a year. Recipients of the letter were asked, if he or she felt disposed to assist the society by joining the orchestra, to write and say so, specifying the instrument.

Charles Smith was gratified with the response, and in January 1879 was able to form from the best of the applicants what he decided to call the Guildhall Amateur Orchestral Society. They had managed to obtain permission to hold their rehearsals free of charge in an empty wool warehouse beside Guildhall at 16 Aldermanbury of which the Corporation were the landlords. They appointed as their conductor the 56-year old violinist whom *Musical Opinion* described as holding 'the uncontested position of the greatest of living English conductors.'

This was Thomas Henry Weist Hill who had been a King's Scholar for the violin at the Royal Academy of Music. During a tour of the United States he had introduced Mendelssohn's Violin Concerto; in 1849 he became a member of Costa's orchestra at the Royal Italian Opera House. He was made director of ballet music at the Theatre Royal Drury Lane in 1871, and between 1874 and 1876 was conductor of the Alexandra Palace orchestra. He was in charge of music at Her Majesty's Theatre until 1879, but at the time he was appointed conductor of the Guildhall Amateur Orchestral Society he was well known to the public as the man responsible for the popular concerts given in the 'empty building' which had once housed the Great Exhibition in Hyde Park now re-erected on the top of Sydenham Hill and popularly dubbed the 'Crystal Palace'. For a time there was a Faculty of Music attached to the Crystal Palace School of Art, Science and Literature to which however only lady students were admitted. Alexandra Palace also had a music school.

The Corporation's role in the establishment of the Orchestral Society by allowing them free use of their property in Aldermanbury was received by the Press as a refreshing change of heart. 'It is gratifying' wrote *The Citizen* in its issue of 19 September 1879, 'to find that the Corporation is occasionally visited with inward stirrings of spirit which have higher aims than paving and drains.' A group formed 'for the cultivation in private City society of the musical art' was welcome. 'The influence of music is universally admitted to be as refining as its cultivation is delightful.'

Obviously the concert in the Mansion House by pupils from Kensington Gore had the desired effect. For on 29 June 1879 the Court of Common Council, on a motion by John Bath, agreed to ask its Music Deputations to consider 'if there be any demand for Musical Education in the City of London such as is supplied at the West End of London, and the best mode of supplying same.'

When, on 19 December, the Deputation met to consider this 'reference', John Bath presented them with a detailed plan for a Corporation School of Music complete with estimates of expense based on a complement of 200 pupils. Moreover he produced a potential list of professors of music prepared to give their services on moderate terms 'in consideration of the object of the Institution'. With memories of the Mansion House concerts by music students still fresh in their minds, and impressed by reports of the response to Charles Smith's appeal to amateur musicians in the City to form an orchestra, they resolved that 'from enquiries made, there is a great demand for musical education in the City of London such as is provided at the West End of London, and that a draft report be prepared in accordance with the suggestion of Mr John Bath'.

Their report was presented to the Court of Common Council on 30 April 1880. It began by recording the establishment of the Guildhall Orchestral and Choral Society 'under the auspices of the Court', which had given the Deputation the opportunity of ascertaining the wants and desires of musical students in connection with the City. The wish of members of the society to attain in a higher degree the knowledge and exercise of the practice and principles of musical science, so as to qualify them to execute well and comprehend fully the works of the great masters, 'was a strong proof that an institution for teaching music thoroughly is most desirable and would be much sought after in the City'.

Additional proof came from the willingness and desire of so many professors of eminence to help with an institution 'which might be made capable not only of competing with the present institutions in the metropolis but also with those in the capitals of other countries'. The impediment so far had been the large expense of obtaining the tuition. 'It is in some measure to remedy this that your deputation propose the establishment of a School of Music in the City of London requiring moderate subvention only.' Payment by pupils should cover payment of the teachers. At first the number of pupils would be strictly limited. The Corporation would only have to pay the Principal and the Secretary, and other incidental expenses, the total not exceeding £350 a year. They recommended that the City Lands Committee be authorised to grant the use of premises at Aldermanbury, part of which were already being used for rehearsals by the Guildhall Orchestral Society. Pupils should be nominated by members of the Court of Common Council and pass an examination as to proficiency, musical talent, degree of aptitude and *disposition to improve under tuition.* Throughout their time at the school pupils would be certified as to assiduity in their studies.

The Court of Common Council accepted the Deputation's report in its entirety, and ordered that steps should be taken at once to put it into effect. It was to be the first municipal school of music in Britain.

Though *Musical Opinion* disliked the idea of students having to obtain the nomination of a common councillor—'we would rather that the tradition of the Circumlocution Office had been dispensed with'—this pioneering action by a body of men hitherto regarded as ultra-conservative and notoriously tight-fisted in regard to anything other than profitable trade and commerce, was welcomed by most of the Press. The prejudice against the establishment of anything so un-English as a department of the fine arts was well known, stated the *Daily Chronicle*, so it congratulated the Common Council for founding a musical academy within the precincts of London with the balance of expenditure over income from fees being met by a sum voted from corporate funds. Most important was the incentive given by the City of London to like action by other towns. 'From the resolution of the public-spirited Common Council a state of things may arise which shall give the musical genius of our people that which it never yet had—a fair chance to develop and assert itself. . . . The spirit in which Lord Chesterfield advised his son neither to play the fiddle himself nor associate with those who did is far from dead. Nor is the feeling extinct which once led society to regard young men and women who devoted themselves to music as persons who had in some sort gone astray from the respectable and dignified paths of life.' Such prejudices could not long survive now. 'Clearly there is a good time coming for the art called divine.'

2 From Aldermanbury to Victoria Embankment

The decision to found the Guildhall School of Music, as the Corporation agreed to call their academy (as opposed to the City School of Music*) was taken at a time of political crisis, which made it all the more praiseworthy. March 1880 saw the surprise dissolution of Parliament. The Conservative prime minister Benjamin Disraeli, now Lord Beaconsfield, warned that those who challenged the expediency of the imperial character of the realm were now attempting to sever the constitutional tie which united Ireland to Great Britain. The electorate would be able to decide upon a course which would materially influence the nation's future fortunes and shape its destiny. 'Rarely in this century' he told the Lords, 'has there been an occasion more critical. The power of England and the peace of Europe will largely depend on the verdict of the country.'

He lost the general election which followed; the Liberals under Mr Gladstone swept the polls—'a startling reverse of fortune' which presumably, however, was more likely to help than hinder the creation of a climate of opinion favourable to the launching of projects such as a new school of music. The Thames Embankment between Blackfriars and Westminster Bridge—a part of London to which this story will shortly relate—was lit with Jablochkoff's electric light by way of celebration.

Not that the flourishing of the arts outside London Wall depended to any great extent on the political state of the country. Throughout

* There was an institution calling itself the 'City School of Music' in Knightrider Street EC4, which had the Bishop of London as its Patron. Its advertisement in the *Musical Times* of October 1892 referred to the school's recent removal to 'new premises'. Dr Henry Wylde had formed the 'London Academy of Music' in 1861. The London Organ School, founded in 1865, was later called The London Music School.

1880 what was called 'English Opera'—*The Bohemian Girl*, *Lily of Killarney*—filled the opera house in Covent Garden; Opera Bouffe the Strand Theatre and the Alhambra—*Fille du Tambour Major*, and other works by Jacques Offenbach who died that very year. Sullivan and Gilbert's latest offering *Pirates of Penzance* played to enthusiastic audiences at the Opera Comique. Mlle Liza Lehmann, 'a soprano with considerable histrionic talent', appeared in *Traviata*. Hubert Parry's *Prometheus Unbound* was given its first performance (at the Gloucester Festival) in 1880; but the most remarkable event of the year according to the Annual Register was Charles Hallé's production of Berlioz's *La Damnation de Faust*. At a Saturday Popular Concert a 'Sextet' for Strings by Anton Dvořák 'a Bohemian composer whose works have attracted the admiration of Brahms and Joachim' met with a favourable reception and 'was afterwards repeated by desire'. At one of these concerts Eugene D'Albert, 'a youthful pianist of great promise', the future composer of the haunting opera *Tiefland*, made his debut in 1880. Herr Richter conducted at the St James's Hall, and Mr Weist Hill at Covent Garden Proms.

It was the latter who, at their meeting of 20 May 1880, the London Corporation's Music Deputation proposed to the Court of Common Council should be appointed 'Director' of the Guildhall School of Music at £150 a year, a recommendation which they endorsed, though the title which Henry Weist Hill assumed was that of Principal. They appointed Charles Smith who had created the Orchestral Society as paid Secretary in charge of administration and his wife as Lady Superintendent. An advertisement inviting applications for tuition at the Guildhall School 'under the conduct and control of the Corporation of the City of London' appeared in newspapers and music journals in July signed 'Frederick A. Catty, Hon. Teacher'. All applicants were personally examined by Henry Weist Hill.

The fees the successful candidates were asked to pay were very much less than those demanded at Kensington Gore or Hanover Square: one guinea a term for one weekly lesson by the 'cheapest' teacher, up to seven guineas a term for four lessons a week (two on the principal subject, one in harmony, one in sight singing) from an 'advanced' teacher. This cost—very low at the time—and the fact that the Guildhall School intended to open in the evening to suit City day-time workers, distinguished the Aldermanbury school from the West

End academies as a place essentially for the amateur, and as much for the encouragement of musical appreciation as the production of teachers and performers. As the Music Deputation were never at loss to point out, good musical education in London was normally very costly 'and the result has been that many persons are employed in teaching who may have some facility in the exercise of the manual part of that so-called profession, but little if any in the fundamental principles of the art they profess to teach'. They saw their school as making redundant poorly qualified teachers in the suburbs who charged would-be violinists and piano players a guinea for a course of twelve lessons given in the pupils' homes. Qualified professors who had agreed to teach pupils at Aldermanbury would save the time and cost of travelling from house to house, which meant they could earn between £500 and £1,000 a year by charging half the price they had to charge for private lessons.

Another distinctive aspect of the Guildhall School was its connection with the Corporation-sponsored Guildhall Orchestral and Choral Society whose Governors were the members of the Music Deputation. The Chairman of the Governors was Polydore De Keyser. Orchestral instrument students were entitled to attend orchestral 'practices'. The orchestra of 97 players and the choir of 120, under the direction of Henry Weist Hill, gave concerts mostly in its warehouse room in Aldermanbury, but also in Guildhall itself. Its inaugural concert took place in the Egyptian Hall at the Mansion House.

It was an attractive formula and was obviously to the taste of the City's amateur music population. Some 62 enrolled for the first term which opened on Monday 27 September 1880. The academic year was to be composed of three terms, each of 13 weeks, and starting on the third Monday of September, January and April. The hours were from 8.30 in the morning to 9.30 at night. Singing teachers included Dr W. H. Cummings and one William Shakespeare (who was conductor of the RAM Choir). Weist Hill taught the violin; Dr John Stainer the organ; Alfred Nelson elocution. There were teachers for the cello, double bass, flute, oboe, clarinet, bassoon, horn, trumpet, trombone, harmonium, harp, harmony and composition. The warehouses at 16 Aldermanbury had been converted into 12 classrooms each with a grand piano and a thermometer; two large rooms for sight singing, harmony lectures and the rest; a large hall for orchestral and choral practice; and administrative offices for Principal Weist Hill and

Secretary Smith. The latter was resident, but with Mrs Charles Smith being Lady Superintendent, his quarters were not entirely private. 'While waiting for their lessons' ran a descriptive piece in *The London Figaro*, 'the young ladies sat in Mrs Smith's drawing room reading, needle working or chatting to one another or to Mrs Smith'—and of course all very elaborately dressed in the long, formal costumes of the day.

It was a good beginning, and at the meeting of 20 December the Music Deputation passed a well-deserved vote of thanks to Robert Parker Taylor who had been chairman in the year the Guildhall School was established. It was an institution, they said, with which his name would always be honourably associated. In the following February came the first offer of an annual prize—from a Lady Jenkinson of £5 for the best performance of Mozart's Piano Concerto in D Minor ('Reinecke edition, no cadenza'). The Principal's salary was doubled. On Thursday evening at 7.30 on 17 March 1881 the School's first Students Concert was held in the Practice Room at Aldermanbury. Gertrude Mary Porter opened it by playing Gounod's *Ave Maria* on the violin, accompanied by Professor Josiah Pittman on the harmonium, and Miss Arnold on the harp. There were pieces on the piano and cello, and songs. The concerts were to be fortnightly, and the next one, on 31 March, opened with a piano duet 'Notturno' written by Herr Carl Mangold and played by his pupils, the brothers Willicombe Mason. The third concert included a New Song composed by student Harriet Kendal called *Out in the Street* and sung by Ellen Marchant. Alice Gough sang Sterndale Bennett's *May Dew*.

The initial intake soon swelled to three figures. By the end of the first term (Autumn 1880) lessons had been given to 246 students. In the first full year (1881) there was an average of 579 a term. Over the next four years the average attendance per term rose from 1,349 (1882) to 2,539 (1885). For the last year at Aldermanbury the average was 2,522 (1886). Attendance had more than quadrupled in six years and fees were bringing in nearly £19,000 a year.

The teaching staff grew accordingly. By the end of 1881 there were 17 teachers of solo singing including Isidore de Lara, Albert Visetti, and J. B. Welch, with Signor Tartaglioni for *solfeggi*. Victoria Bath, daughter of John Bath, was one of 26 piano teachers; there were six teaching harmony and composition; five the organ; two the harp;

five the violin; two the cello; one the double bass; two the flute; one each for the oboe, clarinet, bassoon, horn, trumpet and cornet, ophicleide, sight singing and elocution. A baron taught Italian elocution; a doktor German. 'The Guildhall School' wrote *The World* of 12 October 1881, 'founded on a solid basis, intrusted to a man who deserves, both as a musician and as a gentleman, all possible confidence, has, in the short time of one year, shown power of vitality and development which encourages the best hope for its future achievements.' The first year culminated in a performance in Guildhall of Handel's *Messiah*. The *London Figaro* said it would be almost unique in the history of music in Britain. The 14 principal soloists were all students; all concerned were amateurs connected with a single institution not yet two years old, which had been created by 'practical men of business.' The concert given before the Lord Mayor of London on 17 December 1881 was a joint effort of students of the Guildhall School and members of the band and choir of the Guildhall Orchestral and Choral Society.

Elocution had been in the syllabus from the beginning, but it was only part of learning how to sing, just as The Dramatic Institute proposed by Professor Henry Morley, also in 1880, and simultaneously advocated by the leading actor Sir John Hare, 'for aid to the liberal training of young Actors', would have included lessons in singing. That Morley's idea was not taken up was probably responsible for accelerating, in the quarter of a century which lapsed before Sir Beerbohm Tree launched his experimental academy at His Majesty's Theatre, the process by which the Guildhall School's Elocution Class became one for Dramatic Instruction.

With the patent success of the enterprise of which he was the originator, John Bath was encouraged to persuade the Music Deputation to ask the Common Council for a grant of £200 for scholarships to 'deserving pupils' of the Guildhall School, and for permission to seek donations for other scholarships from the City Livery Companies. The Court agreed. In a leader commenting on this the *Daily Telegraph* pointed out that 'musical genius has, for the most part, had a lowly origin, and either worked on unrecognised after death or early came to the front by the aid of discerning friends'. Haydn was the son of a nobleman's servant; Schubert's father was a poor schoolmaster; Schumann's a country bookseller; Wagner's a civil servant. The writer anticipated 'a possible reaction from the present tendency to undervalue all things English in music'.

> Such a reaction may be imminent, for none of us can have remained unconscious of a stirring in the 'valley of dry bones' and of a waking up to artistic life. There could be no greater proof of stirring and awakening than the action of the City Corporation in first founding, and now endowing with scholarships, a school of music.

The popularity of the Guildhall School was highlighted by the sorry demise of the National Training School for Music in Kensington Gore. It never managed to achieve its ambitious objects, and in 1882 it was re-structured as the Royal College of Music, which took over all the valuable assets and building of the National Training School and was opened by the Prince of Wales on 7 May 1883. The Royal Academy of Music however acquired new confidence. In 1880 it inaugurated the scheme for Local Examinations which had far-reaching effects on musical education generally, along with a system of Metropolitan Examinations for teachers. It published its prize list for the first time in 1882 and two years later held its first public prize giving at the St James's Hall. At the end of the decade the two West End academies formed a Combined Scheme, 'The Associated Board of the RAM and RCM', whose examinations soon justified themselves by extending their operations all over the world.

But not all believed that the Guildhall School of Music was as successful as the Music Deputation, which changed its name to the Music Committee on 26 January 1882, claimed it to be. At the meeting of the Court of Common Council on 18 July 1882 to approve payment of an excess of expenditure over income of £1,104, Councillor Henry Hicks described the Music Committee's report of December 1881 as 'monstrous and untrue'. It was no use to mince matters he said, the Music Committee had been guilty of deception and extravagance; the musical education they had established at the school was but of a mediocre nature; there had been jobbery. The Committee had obtained the Court's consent to its recommendations under false pretences. 'These are strong terms, and I am willing to bear the blame if I do not establish them.' The report showed annual expenses to be £2,043 which was 'an absolute falsehood'.

'With regard to the mediocrity of the education, it has been said that it is my desire to destroy this school. Nothing is further from the truth.' It was doing good work, but should to some extent be self-supporting. Was the Court aware that some 30 professionals had been employed and paid as bassoons, horns and violinists, at each of the concerts widely proclaimed as 'all-amateur'? Few members of the Committee attended meetings; no alderman had ever attended. It was mainly four Councillors who did the business and made the decisions, J. Cox, J. Bath, R. P. Taylor, and Mr Beard. Two of these, Bath and Cox, had appointed their daughters as assistant professors in receipt of pay from pupils [sensation]. It was in contravention of the Council's 81st Standing Order. Thirty one pounds had been paid to the chairman of the Committee in six lots for petty expenses without a voucher. The auditors were Bath and Cox.

This was heady stuff for the newspapers, and the *City Press* made great game of the appointment of Bessie Cox and Victoria Bath as assistant professors, though a student who wished to remain anonymous at once wrote the editor a letter to say he was enjoying a better musical education at Aldermanbury than he had previously received at a West End college at less than half the price. The secret of the City School's success was its central position. *Funny Folks* dismissed the 'Trouble at the Guildhall School' with the comment that it was a trombone of contention that professionals had to be engaged to help at concerts.

But the Music Committee took Henry Hicks's outburst with due seriousness and went into secret session, the minutes of which, they decided, should not be entered in their regular Minute Book but be written separately for their eyes only. When Hicks was called in and questioned, he stuck to his guns. The Town Clerk gave his written opinion that the 81st Standing Order had not been breached. This stated: 'No son of any member of the Court shall be admitted a candidate for any office or situation in the gift or appointment of the Court or any committee or commission of the Court.' The professorships were not paid out of the City's cash and were not appointments within the meaning of the Order. When the Committee moved that the City Solicitor's opinion be sought, they tied, and the chairman gave his casting vote against. John Cox denied all knowledge of his daughter's application.

Once the Special Sub-Committee appointed to report on Henry Hicks's accusations had heard the case of all the 'accused', they jibbed formally at passing judgement, merely minuting that they had resolved 'to forbear from expressing any opinion upon the facts above recorded'. But Hicks's uncompromising comments had their effect, and the newly named Music Committee applied themselves to giving to so un-English and un-City a matter as Musical Education a more responsible approach by immediately drawing up a properly thought out Scheme for the management both of the School and the Orchestral and Choral Society. The Court of Common Council told them that in future they would subsidise the School up to £1,500 a year but no more, exclusive of rent. The Corporation had spent £6,236 on the School to date, and £400 a year on the National Training School scholarships.

The Music Committee made a budget to conform with these figures, and renewed their appeal to the 77 Livery Companies, of whom only the Salters Company had shown any interest by agreeing in July 1882 to give two exhibitions at ten guineas each. Other gifts came in kind. Thomas Chappell presented sheet music. Brinsmeads made a gift of one of their pianos. But neither of these would help pay the Principal's salary which was raised to £800 a year. No one gave them an organ, and concerts were held to raise enough money to buy one. In the meantime lessons were given on the organ in the church across the street.

The main worry that summer of 1882 was not lack of funds but lack of space. Few were deterred by Councillor Hicks's strictures. The School had given lessons to 340 in the Christmas Term of 1880, with a waiting list of 200, and the pressure had never stopped. If anyone was in doubt about the quality of the teaching and the ability of the students to absorb it, he had only to attend a students' performance at Aldermanbury or outside the City at Epping Forest, Bexley Heath, Reading or elsewhere to appreciate that the standard was high. The School's first excursion into the world of opera was the staging on 3 May 1882 of Mendelssohn's *Son and Stranger* (written in 1829 but not published or performed in his lifetime). In June an anthem composed by a student, who had had no training in harmony or composition before entering the School, was performed in St Paul's Cathedral.

By June 1882 the premises in Aldermanbury had become wholly inadequate. The professor who taught the drums had to give his lessons in the coal cellar. As John Bath pointed out in a letter to *The Citizen*, anyone who went there would find warehouses 'tortured in every possible way from their original intention by the skill of an architect in a vain attempt to make them answer a purpose for which they were never intended and upon which nearly seven hundred pounds have already been expended'. The lath and plaster partitions with glass upper parts were altogether too thin and had no sound insulation. Trombone playing in one classroom ruined the piano lesson next door. One of the suggestions was that students should be allowed to practise in rooms in the new Law Courts which had recently been opened in the Strand opposite Temple Bar. Return to the previous idea of coming to an arrangement with Gresham College? But the *City Press* (17 June) reflected the general opinion that that institution had become a 'byword for slothfulness and uselessness'. Move to the City of London School building in Honeypot Lane which was soon to become vacant? Probably the best course would be to explore further the Court of Common Council's request to the City Lands Committee of 7 July 1881 to examine the possibility of using a plot owned by the Corporation on Thames Embankment. It would certainly be inconsistent with the new businesslike image of the reformed Music Committee to go on spending more money on the converted warehouse.

The pressure on space was relaxed, at least, by absentees or when a pupil suddenly found herself unable to complete the course and had to leave the School prematurely. Such was the case of the 16-year old Beatrice Tanner who had just spent an exciting 1881 in Paris with her Aunt Kate, and had come back to her home in Dulwich where she spent the long evenings 'either at the piano or playing chess or listening to my mother singing to her guitar'.

When the former Miss Tanner wrote her autobiography some years later, she remembered the events of 1881:

'On my return from Paris, a cousin of my father, Mrs Eliza Hogarth, a woman of some means, heard me play the piano, and offered to have me trained. So it was arranged that I should go to the Guildhall School of Music twice a week, from Dulwich, for my lesson. After the second term my Music Master suggested that I should go in, with 365 other girls, for a scholarship which would give me three years free musical tuition in Leipzig. I won the scholarship; why I never took it up belongs to another chapter. The following letter from my Music Master, Mr Ridley Prentice, shows that I had a little musical talent.'

My dear Madam,

I much regret to find from your daughter, Miss Beatrice Tanner, that she will leave the Guildhall School of Music at the half term. Personally, I shall be very sorry to lose her as a pupil, as she is much interested in her work, has great talent and makes rapid progress. But I feel that, quite apart from my personal feeling, it is my duty to let you know what a very serious thing it seems to me that Miss Tanner should not complete her musical education.

When she came to me, she had never had any regular musical training at all, and there was much to undo before she could really begin to make sure progress. She has now got over that first difficulty, and there is nothing to stop her from becoming a really fine pianist and musician—but this of course is a work of time and labour and cannot be accomplished all at once.

I have no hesitation in saying that she has a very great talent indeed, and that if she works in a proper spirit, and is properly directed, she is sure of attaining a very high position. It seems to me therefore that it would be a *wrong* thing if such talent were not to be properly developed, especially as in the present day no one has any chance of success who has not attained the highest possible point.

You will see that I look upon the matter as a musician. Doubtless there are many other different considerations which must weigh with you, but I trust that you will pardon my writing strongly. It is not often that one meets with real talent, so that it is all the more sad when there seems to be a prospect of its being wasted. Perhaps I may be allowed to add that the very great pains which I have taken with Miss Tanner give me a right to speak.

Believe me, dear Madam,
Yours sincerely,

Ridley Prentice

The reason why Beatrice Tanner never took up her scholarship to Leipzig was that she had fallen in love with the good-looking 20-year old Patrick Campbell whose parents lived at Sydenham. But Ridley Prentice's letter did postpone the breaking off of her lessons for six months, and she left the Guildhall School in July 1883. 'We eloped within four months of our first meeting, and were married at St Helens Church, Bishopsgate Street' wrote Mrs Patrick Campbell, the famous actress of 1922, in *My Life and Some Letters*. 'One thing I can never forget—my mother's face and her heartbroken cry when I told her.' She had two children in three years. Patrick's health was failing. 'I knew Pat was not strong enough to continue working in the City and I must help. I could not imagine what work I could do. I had given up my musical scholarship, and so was not qualified for a musical career. My lovely baby, and another coming in a few weeks, must be provided for. I was bewildered—lost.' She soon found her niche however in the Theatre. She made her first professional appearance in Liverpool in 1888; thereafter the talented piano pupil of the Guildhall School of Music would never become a luminary of the concert hall as her teacher had hoped. Patrick Campbell was killed in the Boer War one month after going to South Africa in 1900, and Mrs Patrick Campbell's meteoric career on the stage ended only with her death in 1940.

The number of girls and boys abandoning their lessons for romantic, financial and other reasons was never on a scale, however, to make the Music Committee relax its efforts to solve the space problem. When they heard that 'Mr Architect' was working out a scheme 'for the re-arrangement of courts and offices in and around Guildhall' they discussed with the Special Guildhall Improvement Committee the possibility of this including accommodation for the Guildhall School of Music. When that proved impractical a Sub-Committee of five reviewed sites which had come on the market in Warwick Square and Finsbury, and had a look at the facilities provided by the Royal College of Music in Kensington. But finally they returned to the idea of constructing a new building to cost £18,000 on a 10,000 sq ft site at the Blackfriars end of Victoria Embankment, which would be let to the Music Committee by a syndicate called Ground Rents Limited for 3s a foot super. After a certain amount of bargaining the Committee agreed to take 8,000 ft, with the expectation that they would pay a peppercorn rent for the building to be erected and owned by the Corporation. When the contracts were placed, the ground rent was fixed at £1,100 and the estimated cost of construction had gone up to £19,500.

For the Music Committee the last years at Aldermanbury were spent in a drastic re-thinking of the whole exercise in an earnest attempt to meet Henry Hicks's requirement of near self-sufficiency. They reduced the budget they had proposed for 1883 from £1,900 to £1,470, and planned the increases in income and the reductions in expenditure which would make this possible. The 60 members of the Orchestral Society and 80 members of the Choir would have to pay more subscriptions; and the School would take a percentage of the fees pupils paid to their teachers, which varied according to the teacher's 'rank'. The Committee reckoned these subscriptions and fees would help to meet the Hicks requirement and, indeed, by the end of 1883 they even had a small surplus on them.

Charles Smith, the Secretary, was against economising by reducing the teaching staff. He won. The committee looked at instruments: the School should buy instead of hiring them, as a saving in the long run. So they authorized expenditure to buy a violin, a cello, six double basses, three timpani, a bass drum and two harps. They halved the amount to be spent on the hire of sheet music and reduced the budget for rehearsal expenses. They introduced an examination fee, ordered that classes should be increased from six to eight, and that the total annual intake of paying pupils (excluding 'exhibitioners') should be kept at 1,200.

More members of the Music Committee than ever before—17— attended the important meeting of 20 October 1882 at which these decisions were taken, which was further evidence of the seriousness with which they took the criticisms of Henry Hicks. Some of them, who were probably applying themselves to the matter for the first time, suggested that the City's own music academy should have another name (though the minutes do not state what). But they were overruled, and the majority opted for keeping the name 'Guildhall School of Music', however far from Guildhall the Principal, Henry Weist Hill, with his staff and pupils, might be moving in the near future.

Thomas Henry Weist Hill
The first Principal of the Guildhall School
1880–1892

2. And of late the City has been indebted for its music to foreign Artistes.

3. Professors have offered their services in founding a School of Music.

That the City of London should suddenly concern itself with Musical Education was considered highly humorous by the cartoonists of the 1880s. 'Music in the City' was typical

Punch had to add its comment of course: 'Harmony in the City—at last!'

Mr Miller held the vase while Chairman Morrison placed in it a copy of the *Times* of that day, the *City Press* and the *Citizen*. The City Architect sealed the base and the Chairman put the vase in the well of the stone. The City Architect gave the Chairman the trowel who spread the mortar and the stone was lowered into place. Mr Johnson bore the Square, Mr Beedel the Level, and Mr London the Straight Edge. They gave them to the Chairman who adjusted and set the stone striking it with a mallet presented to him by Mr Beard, and declared the stone to be well and truly laid. Rev Prebendary Whittington, Rector of St Peter's Cornhill, offered prayer, and then all separated.

Thus, on 21 July 1885, was laid the foundation stone of the new Guildhall School of Music which was to occupy about a third of the island site bounded by John Carpenter Street, Tallis Street, Carmelite Street, and Tudor Street, within 200 yards of the Victoria Embankment. It was then at the end of Tallis Street, the entrance overlooking the river Thames and its John Carpenter Street side facing the Corporation's City of London School for Boys, which had opened only three years before.

Some said that the new music school was being erected on the foundations of the Duke's Theatre in Dorset Gardens which Sir William Davenant had built in 1668 'a little south of Old Salisbury Court and close to the River' (before the Embankment was built). It was certainly near enough, and appropriate as Davenant was England's first opera impresario. But, as the section of the 1875 Ordnance Survey Map shows, the Guildhall School of Music was a few yards to the west of the Duke's Theatre site which was (and is) occupied by the playground of the Boys' School. The area had a distinguished musical history all around it. The Temple lawyers to the west had been prominent in the development of Elizabethan drama. To the north, the lutenist songwriters of Jacobean times all lived and worked near St Dunstan's in Fleet Street. John Banister started the first concerts in Britain where the audience—the general public—paid at the door. His house off Tudor Street, he announced, was

now called the Musick School, over against the George Tavern in White Fryers; this present Monday will be musick performed by excellent masters, and at 4 o'clock every afternoon. (1672)

The immediately previous occupier of the land on which the foundation stone of a new 'Musick School' was being laid 300 years

35

later was the less romantic Retort House and gasometers of a Gas Works.

John Carpenter Street was named after the 15th-century Town Clerk of Lord Mayor Dick Whittington. On his death in 1442, John Carpenter bequeathed certain of his landed properties to the City Corporation and willed that from the profits of these estates it should educate and maintain four boys born within the City—'Carpenter's Children'. From this benefaction sprang the City of London School for Boys built in 1837 under the shadow of St Paul's Cathedral on the site of the old Honey Lane Market in Milk Street, moving to John Carpenter Street in 1882. The Milk Street school was only demolished in 1955. The Guildhall School in Blackfriars still stood empty and grey in 1980.

It seems that those who were formulating plans for a music school in the City benefited from the experience of those who had hoped, but failed, to found a Handel College in 1859 to mark the centenary of the composer's death. This was to have been an orphanage for the children of musicians whose education would doubtless have included music lessons. In the 1860s, a certain Owen Jones (whose descendants have designed many a City building since) gave a site worth £5,000 and his services as an architect for the Handel College. (Dr Charles Burney had championed a similar idea almost a hundred years earlier.) 'What happened to this grand scheme is not to be learnt from the Musical Times', wrote Percy Scholes in *The Mirror of Music 1844–1944*, vol. II, 'but Novello's *Short History of Cheap Music* (p. 79) asserts that "a great portion of the details prepared for the College was used in the construction of the Guildhall School of Music a quarter of a century later".'

While the new building was under construction the Music Committee busied themselves with the choice and ordering of equipment. The Corporation's Coal, Corn and Finance Committee wanted the budget for furniture and fittings reduced. A fireproof floor for the Practice Room however was obligatory, and they were not to be deprived of their mosaic pavement in the corridors. It was a question of spreading the allocation as well as they could on the bells and speaking tubes, the fenders, umbrella stands and shoe scrapers; the noiseless linoleum for 50 rooms ('the material to be with a fancy border'): the 50 clocks ('the cases to be of oak'); the 40 coal boxes; the window blinds of plain brown holland; the small rugs to go under the

Certificates of Proficiency had been awarded since 1885—Minnie Hailstone was the first to be given one—and the Prospectus of June 1891 listed 15 'Associates and Holders of Certificates of Proficiency' and 203 'Holders of Certificates of Merit', which were introduced in 1887 with May Elliott heading the list. On payment of an examination fee any pupil who had been three years in the School could ask to be examined for a Certificate of Proficiency and an Associateship of the Guildhall School of Music; the entrance fee was less for a Certificate of Merit. No one was allowed to announce himself as 'of the Guildhall School of Music' unless he held at least one of these certificates.

No member could be selected to take part in one of the School concerts unless he or she had been a pupil for at least two terms; ladies of the choir and orchestra were required to wear white dresses.

Henry Weist Hill, the School's first Principal, was taken ill in March 1890 and was given three months' leave of absence. He never returned and died on 26 December 1891. The staff petitioned the Music Committee 'not to make selection of Principal outside the School' but to no avail. There were 16 applicants for the position including Orton Bradley, Musical director of the People's Palace in Whitechapel, and William Carter, director of the National Concerts at the Albert Hall. From a short list of Sir William Cusins, Master of Music to Queen Victoria, Thomas Wingham and Sir Joseph Barnby, the Corporation chose the last who took up his duties in April 1892. The opportunity was taken of making the Principal of the Guildhall School an Officer of the Corporation of London under the 13th Standing Order, and they fixed his salary at £1,000.

The scene in John Carpenter Street on 21 July 1885 when Pearse Morrison, chairman of the London Corporation's Music Committee which sponsored the Guildhall School of Music, laid the foundation stone of the new building to which the school was to move from its first premises at 16 Aldermanbury behind Guildhall.

The Tallis Street entrance view of the 1886 School from Victoria Embankment.

Drama as well as Music was being taught at the Guildhall School as early as 1887, though they called it 'Elocution'— a tradition that had not entirely disappeared in 1980.

Hats and skirts to the ankle were *de rigueur* for pupils of the Guildhall School of 1887.

Sir Joseph Barnby
The second Principal of the Guildhall School
1892–1896

Dr W H Cummings
The third Principal of the Guildhall School
1896–1910

The double doors of the classrooms at the new Guildhall School in John Carpenter Street were for sound insulation, and the glazed panels for the protection of professors against hysterical pupils, and of pupils against attentions which were not in the curriculum.

3 William Cummings gets his Theatre

54-year old Joseph Barnby had been in the choir of York Minster and at the age of 12 been appointed Assistant Organist. In 1854 he became a student of the Royal Academy of Music in London—the 14-year old Arthur Sullivan beat him for the Mendelssohn Scholarship—and for a while he was organist at St Anne's, Soho. In 1872 he was conducting orchestral concerts at the St James's Hall and the Exeter Hall, and succeeded Gounod as conductor of the Royal (Albert Hall) Choral Society. For 17 years he was Precentor and Director of Musical Instruction at Eton College. A composer of oratorios, cantatas, hymns and anthems, he was musical adviser to Novello, Ewer & Co, the music publishers, whose offer to sell to the Guildhall School their library of music valued at ten thousand dollars was declined. He received his knighthood in 1892, the year of his new appointment.

Sir Joseph was happy to let the immediate arrangements of his predecessor run their course. The Orchestra and Choir gave a fine performance of Arthur Sullivan's *Golden Legend* in the St James's Hall; and students of the Opera Class gave their first *public* performance on 10 May 1892 at the Lyric Theatre—*Fra Diavolo*. That December they mounted a production of *The Marriage of Figaro*. All this pointed to the need for a 'Stage Director', and at the end of 1894 Giulia Warwick was appointed 'Professor of Operatic Deportment and General Stage Training' for ladies. Giulia had been a member of the Carl Rosa Company, and had been in the original cast of Gilbert and Sullivan's *The Sorcerer*. There were still regular concert performances such as that of Berlioz's *Faust* in the Queen's Hall, at the end of which Sir Joseph Barnby, the conductor, having been taken ill halfway through, collapsed.

Links now began to be forged with the lighter side of music, the theatre of the lower brow associated with the names of George Edwardes and Augustus Harris, friends of whom presented the

Guildhall School (and the other two schools), as a tribute to their work for 'English Opera', with a Steinway grand piano to be competed for by students. One girl, Norah Girton, was engaged by Mr D'Oyly Carte as a member of the Royal English Opera company while still a student at John Carpenter Street, and then George Edwardes cast her as Juliette in *A Gaiety Girl* and in a pantomime at the Theatre Royal, Bath. It was a trend not altogether to the liking of the Music Committee, whose chairman, T. H. Ellis, protested to the Court of Common Council that girls who came to the Guildhall School no longer became prima donnas, only chorus girls.

There were some who thought the School was mistaken in attempting anything too sophisticated. When a cast of students gave Gounod's *Romeo and Juliet* in English at the Drury Lane Theatre, the music critic of the *Daily Telegraph* questioned the advisability of 'soaring rashly into the regions of 5-act opera' and 'turning loose a number of budding young artists with all their imperfections on their heads, and allowing them to render an immature and often ludicrous account of an exacting opera in a theatre as large as Drury Lane'. But Labouchère's normally abrasive *Truth* attacked those who had criticised the Drury Lane production, and asserted that the foundation of the Guildhall School of Music was one of the most useful pieces of educational work which the London Corporation had ever done.

It was an opinion echoed by the celebrated Dr Hans Richter who paid the School a visit in the summer of 1895 and praised everything he saw. (He will have met several fellow-countrymen including the distinguished German violinist Wilhelmj who taught at the School between 1893 and 1908, and Wilhelm Ganz, pianist and violinist, who was also a teacher of singing.) At the prizegiving that year Sir Joseph Barnby said the School now occupied a proud and unrivalled position. 'In the future history of music in this country the work done at this institution will have to be reckoned with.' At the annual dinner given by the Music Committee at the Albion Tavern in December W. T. Roberts reminded the gathering that when they first mooted the idea of a School of Music they were regarded as faddists. 'But now the Corporation has done more for music than any other municipality in the world.'

The most characteristic feature of the School, wrote Sir Joseph in an article in *The Strand Musical Magazine* that year, was that while the majority of the great music schools of Britain devoted their energies to the training of professional musicians, the Guildhall School offered its advantages equally to those who were likely to form future audiences.

> The benefit resulting from this spread of musical knowledge amongst amateurs will not be far to seek. The young people of today will be the heads of families in the next generation, and they will not only be able to enjoy music with a more intelligent and cultivated mind themselves, but in turn will be able to exercise greater discrimination in the selection of teachers, and in deciding on the course of study of their children.

Together the three schools of music in London were turning out 500 pupils a year, of which the mainly amateur output from Victoria Embankment was the largest. More than three thousand took lessons every term at the Guildhall which was now very nearly self-supporting.

Though definitely a poor relation, the teaching of Dramatic Art kept its place in the curriculum, and at the end of 1894 broke out of the purely operatic mould with an 'Elocutionary and Dramatic Recital' featuring scenes from Shakespeare's *Merchant of Venice* and Sheridan's *School for Scandal*, the first of many under the new professor Allen Beaumont, who had been associated with Henry Irving at the Lyceum. Many who were to become stars of the stage however came to the School not to join the Dramatic Art classes, but to learn the piano. One such was Dame Sybil Thorndike who started taking lessons at the age of 12 in 1894. In an article she wrote for the first issue of *The Guildhall Music Student* in 1924 she said that some of the happiest days of her life had been spent at the Guildhall School of Music. 'I think the spirit of the School got into our bones. It was a very hardworking, immensely stimulating atmosphere to be in.' She took lessons from Francesco Berger who was with the School for 40 years and was in the habit of rewarding good playing with sandwiches out of his luncheon box. Sybil Thorndike remembered the prize coming her way for a better than usual rendering of a Polonaise by Chopin. She got her first enthusiasm for counterpoint from Professor Greenish— 'a balancing, steadying, most absorbing study which can give one a rest that extra sleep can never give'. Bessie Cox taught her things which were of great service to her in her acting career. Her brother Frank was also a pupil, learning the cello from Ebenezer Prout.

Both composer and librettist personally supervised the final rehearsals of a private production by the Operatic Class of *Princess Ida* which took place in the Practice Room on 19 December 1895 conducted by Sir Joseph Barnby. The Principal had never fully recovered from the symptoms which had caused his collapse at the Queen's Hall though he had returned in April, and been presented with a grandfather clock and other gifts by students and staff to mark the event. In January 1896, he died. Sir Arthur Sullivan and Sir Augustus Harris were pallbearers at his funeral, the last part of which was held in St Paul's. His death took the Music Committee unawares, and in the five month interregnum which followed the Secretary, Hilton Carter, acted as Principal in all but name.

Only 12 applied for the post in the first instance, but when the Music Committee extended the time limit they had applications from 35. The voting (out of the short list presented to the Court of Common Council by the Music Committee) was held in public, with the two finalists addressing their case to the 173 councillors. There was 'an unseemly wrangle' over procedure—were councillors to vote for one candidate only, or a first and second choice? The names of all applicants had been published in the Press and their respective chances of election widely debated. The *Saturday Review* backed Dr Turpin, but when the voting took place in June a majority of 21 (97 to 76) chose Dr W. H. Cummings who at 65 was older than the man he was succeeding. For some time he had been on the teaching staff.

William Cummings's father had been head verger at St Paul's and he himself had been a cathedral chorister. For many years he had been the tenor most in demand at British music festivals and concerts for oratorios and the rest. He was not only a fine singer but also a composer and writer on music. His cantata *The Fairy Ring* had met with wide acclaim and he had written a useful *Primer of the Rudiments of Music* as well as a *Life of Purcell* which, when its own candidate was rejected, the *Saturday Review* described as 'singly ill-written'. The English musical world however welcomed the appointment, and at a banquet to mark the occasion at the Hotel Cecil in July the principal guests included Dr Hubert Parry, Sir John Stainer and Dr Frederick Bridge, the new conductor of the Royal Choral Society. William Cummings, said Sir A. C. Mackenzie who took the chair, was a man of spotless integrity, of calm, dispassionate judgement and a trusty, genial friend.

The new broom at once set about revising the examination system which he divided into three grades, Primary, Intermediate and Advanced. He abolished Certificates of Proficiency and introduced a fourth grade which entitled a student to become an 'Associate' of the School, the examination for which was held only once a year in July for students at the end of their third year. This put the Guildhall School of Music's examination at one with those of the Royal Academy of Music and the Royal College of Music (though they alone had the right to grant degrees in Music, along with the universities and the Archbishop of Canterbury). With the introduction of the AGSM, the School became a diploma-conferring institution. This led to a proposal that the Guildhall School should combine with the RAM, the RCM and the Trinity College of Music (founded in 1872) as the Faculty of Music in a University of Westminster—but nothing came of it.

Cummings's main problem was the recurring one of over-crowding —they now had to accommodate 3,000 students a term—and he instigated a serious study of how best the School could physically expand. The main handicap was having no sizeable theatre and being so dependent on the Great Hall of the City of London School. Cummings was keen to develop 'straight' drama, and not all that classical either; while the Opera Class's Christmas production at the Lyceum was Flotow's *Martha*, he gave all support to his new drama teacher L. F. Chapuy in his production of J. B. Burkstone's farce *Mischief Making* in the Practice Room.

He wanted a *theatre* which could be both an opera house and a playhouse, and the centrepiece of a School of Dramatic Instruction. He toured the continent of Europe to see their drama schools and gave a full account of his requirements to the City Architect who was to design the 'annexe' which the Corporation agreed to build at a cost of £22,000 on the land adjoining the existing building. Henry Weist Hill had purposely kept this vacant against the day when the City guilds could be persuaded to subscribe enough money to fill it. When Mr Deputy Pearse Morrison, once more Chairman of the Music Committee, laid the foundation stone of the new wing in July 1897 he said the ground floor would house what he called a commodious Orchestral Saloon to hold 650, with a properly equipped stage, and 30 new classrooms on the second, third and fourth floors. Cummings made it plain that he saw the extension as the means of enabling the institution to offer the facilities of a Dramatic School, and not restricted to performance of dramatic opera. The stage was to be a small reproduction of that at Her Majesty's Theatre in the Haymarket, and decorated by J. M. Boekbinder who had transformed the interiors of the Theatre Royal, Drury Lane and the Alhambra. It had electric lighting 'superior to any other in England'. The lights on the stage could be dimmed 'by an ingenious patent' instead of having to switch them off one by one. 'We are about to try the experiment of giving a thorough training in everything that pertains to the art of acting as soon as our new theatre is built and ready for use' he told the *Musical Times* (28 May 1898). 'It has long been an ambition of mine to do something of the kind.' So far such instruction as had been given was 'very unreal'. They had no proper theatre; no stage. They had had to mark entrances and exits on the floor in chalk. Sir Henry Irving had allowed students to rehearse in the Lyceum Theatre—but only once. At the end of their musical education many pupils received good chances from Mr D'Oyly Carte and others, but they first had to learn how to walk the stage and dispose of their hands and limbs gracefully. Up to now they could only do so by going into the chorus or as 'walking gentlemen', and their voices were injured as a result. Once the Guildhall School had its own theatre, they would have a Stage Director and professors of deportment, dancing and fencing, and a Chorus Master and a prompter. There would be compulsory rehearsals, and students would learn the discipline of the professional theatre. 'Everything will be carried on seriously and without caprice of any kind.' Many had written to him to approve of his plans, and he had had encouragement from Sir Henry Irving, George Alexander and Sir Beerbohm Tree, who he hoped would become honorary examiners.

The extension was opened by the Lord Mayor of London on 11 July 1898 and the first performances in the new theatre were Gounod's *The Mock Doctor*, conducted by Ernest Ford, and Mr Chapuy's production of *The Winter's Tale* preceded by a curtain-raiser *For Cyril's Sake*. The Guildhall School of Music entered on a new lease of life.

To the building in John Carpenter Street off Victoria Embankment to which the Guildhall School moved in 1886 (left) was added in 1898 the extension seen on the right, which included a theatre in which students could perform opera and stage plays.

The stage of the theatre in the extension to the Guildhall School opened in 1898 had this ornate proscenium, surmounted by the arms of the City of London, modelled on Her Majesty's Theatre.

to produce composers was demonstrated when the gold medallist of 1899, 24-year old H. Waldo Warner, wrote the music of a comic opera called *The Royal Vagrants*, A Story of Conscientious Objection, which was performed in the School theatre, with himself conducting, in July 1900.

For students without the financial backing of well-to-do parents, raising the money for the entrance fees and tuition fees presented a serious problem. Young Carrie Tubb, one of eight children, turned to making frocks for her friends to pay for the singing lessons which she started having from Frederick Birch in 1901. 'You had to have a fighting instinct to succeed as a singer, not just a voice' she recollected in 1927. After singing Beethoven's 'Ah, Perfido!' in the School concert, she joined the Opera Class and played Kate in Goetz's opera *The Taming of The Shrew* which made an impression few forgot. But thoughts of an immediate operatic career had to be abandoned when, soon after leaving the School, she fell off her bicycle and injured her spine. She then married and had a son, and only returned to professional singing some time later. She made her debut at Covent Garden in 1910, to become one of the great singers and teachers in her long association with the School. She died, aged 100, in 1978.

The Dramatic Instruction classes trained people to take their place in the Theatre other than as performers. In 1904 George Barrington, one time student, became Manager of the Theatre Royal, Drury Lane. In the same year Cairns James, who was a professor at John Carpenter Street, founded his own School of Musical and Dramatic Art at 77 New Oxford Street which, alas, did not long survive; and Sir Beerbohm Tree founded the Royal Academy of Dramatic Art at His Majesty's Theatre, moving the next year to Gower Street where it still flourishes. Four years later still Elsie Fogerty founded the Central School of Speech Training and Dramatic Art at the Albert Hall. The Guildhall School shed its Elocution and Gesture Class image with the appointment as Professor of Dramatic Art in 1906 of 40-year old Kate Rorke who had been on the stage since 1878 and leading lady for many of the outstanding actor-managers of the day, including Sir John Hare, Sir George Alexander, Lewis Waller and Sir Beerbohm Tree, with whom she toured America. 'My object' she said, 'will not be to teach people to elocute and gesticulate but to put them through a course of rehearsals.' Her first productions in the School theatre were W. S. Gilbert's 3-act fairy play *Broken Hearts* and Sydney Grundy's

Man Proposes. In 1906 a prize was presented for fencing—the Alliston Fencing Prize.

Cummings saw that lectures as well as plays and concerts (of which the School's thousandth was given in 1904) took place in the School. The first of the series he instituted was given by Sir Frederick Bridge of London University on the Value of Degrees in Music. When George Bernard Shaw was one of ten speakers at a conference held in the School by the London Shakespeare League, a man in the audience rose to object to 'GBS' being allowed to speak. The playwright had insulted Henry Irving by claiming the actor had asked for a title in 1895. Shaw said he bore no grudge against Sir Henry but it was a pity he had not encouraged modern dramatists.

It was after Cummings had himself delivered a lecture—to the Incorporated Society of Musicians at Buxton in January 1907—that he found himself the defendant in a libel action. He was a genial, tolerant, untidy, rag-bag of a man, but one thing which roused him above all else was humbug. The famous tenor and Principal of the Guildhall School of Music took the opportunity of the Buxton lecture, at which he knew the Press were present, of exposing as a fraud the Horspool Natural Voice Academy which, in its advertisements and prospectus, guaranteed to give 'all not vocally malformed a perfect singing and speaking voice'. Cummings's caustic ridicule of such a claim was reported in the *Daily Telegraph*, and Joel Horspool issued a writ for libel and slander. At the trial before Mr Justice Darling, Horspool's counsel said Dr Cummings had imputed that his client was an impudent quack, that he and his company imposed on the public and had a fraudulent business. Cummings brought a string of distinguished singers to the witness box to testify that Horspool's claims were outrageous nonsense. The proceedings took four days and the jury five minutes to find for Cummings and award him his costs. At the suggestion of Charles Santley, who was one of his witnesses, his friends presented him with a testimonial during a dinner at the Trinity College of Music. At the Mansion house the next day the Lord Mayor presented him with a cheque for 500 guineas, the proceeds of a fund raised to show the pleasure with which the musical world welcomed his victory, to which the London Corporation gave 50 guineas. It was accompanied by an address signed by 800 professors of music. In the evening there was a banquet in his honour at De Keyser's Royal Hotel. The triumph was complete—except that

Horspool went bankrupt, still owing Cummings his costs.

The strain of the trial took its toll, and at the beginning of 1910 the 79-year old Principal was given several months' leave of absence, which he spent in Devon. He took up his duties again for the autumn term and then announced his retirement (6 October 1910). Under his direction the School's popularity had reached a peak. The greatest achievement of his 14 years as Principal however was persuading the Music Committee to fund the building of the extension with its theatre and seeing the project through to finality. Yet he was not able to prod them into spending money on providing hot water or installing a telephone. The means of communication was by hand-written message delivered by one of eight porters dressed in dark blue uniforms. If they were lucky they could save climbing the stairs by using the hydraulic lift, but its performance was erratic. When it came to giving the retiring Principal a pension however, the Committee generously granted him £500 a year instead of the £300 he was entitled to. Under the leadership of their new chairman, John Pakeman, the Music Committee established nine new scholarships in place of the five recommended by the Special Enquiry Committee, totalling £410 a year, which shamed at least one Livery Company to make good their previous lack of interest in the City's musical education activities. The Grocers Company agreed to found a scholarship. The Music Committee were also persuaded that the time had come positively to advertise the School, and offered a ten-guinea prize to the artist who produced the best poster design, a competition which attracted 200 entries.

John Pakeman, who undertook the duties of Principal until the Common Council had made a new appointment, thought it was unlikely that the dozen or so men in England sufficiently eminent to take over would answer an advertisement, and told the Music Committee that they should select and nominate three from whom the Court of Common Council would make the final choice. On holiday at Blackpool at the time was one L. R. Russell, son of Henry Russell, composer of *A Life on the Ocean Wave* and *Cheer, Boys, Cheer*. Professionally the young Mr Russell used the names represented by his initials, and as 'Landon Ronald' had already acquired an international reputation as accompanist, conductor and master musician. He trained as a pianist and violinist at the Royal College of Music, and when he left after five years he was engaged by Sir

Augustus Harris as second conductor (maestro al piano) at Covent Garden Theatre. He was only 18. He conducted his first public performance there when he was 22. When Harris was asked by Nellie Melba to recommend someone to help her with the score of Massenet's *Manon*, he suggested the young Landon Ronald, who in 1894 became her accompanist and acted as conductor of the orchestra for her American tour of 1895. He was the composer of more than 100 songs of which 'Down In The Forest' achieved the greatest popularity. He added extra numbers in *Floradora* and *Little Miss Nobody*, and wrote incidental music for straight plays like Robert Hichens' *The Garden of Allah*. Through the tenor Paolo Tosti he became a frequent visitor to Windsor Castle as an accompanist; the ageing Queen Victoria was delighted by him. As a conductor he was at first better known abroad than in England. To his own pleasure and surprise, being a Jew did not prevent him achieving success in conducting the Philharmonic Orchestra in Berlin, even then, as he said, 'the very centre of anti-Semitism'. Recognition in England came after he had stood in for Hans Richter and conducted a Philharmonic Society concert in place of the famous German conductor who had been taken ill. 'This was the turning point in my career in London' he wrote in *Myself and Others* (1931). 'It meant everything to me. . . . From this date I never looked back and work simply poured in on me.' He received concert engagements all over Britain . . . and every Sunday at the Albert Hall.

In 1900 he was approached by Barry Owen, managing director of The Gramophone Company in Maiden Lane, to persuade performers to take an interest in the gramophone which till then had been merely a toy for the nursery. By 1900 the new ten-inch records needed first class singers to show off their possibilities. At first he was lukewarm, but when Owen played him a record, to his surprise the reproduction was such that he recognised the voice of a baritone he knew. 'I saw the enormous possibilities at once, but realised equally quickly that I should have to overcome the most tremendous prejudice that existed in the minds of all artists against what was considered by them an outrage on their art.' He persuaded the tenor Ben Davies to make a record and then Calvé. Adelina Patti held out the longest but was finally induced to submit to the ordeal.

Thus the celebrity who was taking a working holiday at Blackpool that summer of 1910 had showed himself to be very much more than the traditional conductor with conventional attitudes. Here was a man anxious to lead his fellow musicians into the new twentieth century, and seize the opportunities it offered. One day he was joined by a friend of his, Max Mossel, a professor at John Carpenter Street, who told him that John Pakeman had been one of the party in a box at Covent Garden the night before and mentioned that he and his Music Committee were looking for a new Principal at the Guildhall School of Music. Mossel said he had taken the liberty of telling Pakeman he thought they could not do better than appoint Landon Ronald whom he happened to be visiting the next day. The famous conductor's first reaction was that on no account would he consider doing any such thing. Mossel insisted that it was only a matter of allowing his name to go forward for consideration by the Court; there could be no harm in meeting Pakeman and hearing what he had to say. The two had dinner at Pakeman's club a few days after Ronald's return to London, and by the end of it he had agreed for his name to go forward.

'This immense rush of work continued unabated until 1910', he recalled in *Myself and Others*, 'when, as a bolt from the blue, I was offered the post of Principal of the Guildhall School of Music, my age being 37. I loved the idea of accepting the offer but I was afraid to do so on account of giving up my work as conductor.' He appeared before the Special Sub-Committee of the Music Committee appointed to nominate the three names. 'Grave objection', he wrote in his earlier memoirs *Variations On A Personal Theme* (1922), 'was taken by this special committee, and later by the grand committee, to my condition that I should be allowed to continue my career as a conductor.' 'Entirely through the kindly offices of my dear friend Sir John Pakeman', he wrote in 1931, 'a *modus operandi* was discovered, and on November 3, 1910 I took up my duties with great and lasting enthusiasm.' They had ruled that he should only undertake work for anyone other than the Corporation of London with the permission of the Music Committee, but made him understand that this would always be freely given. He told them it was his intention to hold the office of Principal for three years only.

Sir Landon Ronald
The fourth Principal of the Guildhall School
1910–1938
(Knighted in 1922)

4 War, Landon Ronald and Wireless

His policy at the Guildhall School, Landon Ronald told the *Daily Mail*, would be 'absolutely modern and progressive'. He proposed taking on staff able to instil into students 'the spirit of modernity as opposed to the old-fashioned views hitherto in vogue in our musical academies'. He would continue conducting the New Symphony Orchestra. He was encouraged by the successes which Guildhall School students were currently enjoying in the professional theatre— Ethel Cadman was leading lady of Mr Frohman's New York *Arcadians* company, Constance Hyem was in *Koffo of Bond Street* at the Palace of Varieties where the conductor Herman Finck was an ex-pupil too. Kate Rorke was an active professional like himself, doubling her duties as Drama Professor with appearing nightly in *The Toymaker of Nuremburg*. This enabled him and her to find work for talented students when they left the School. It compelled them 'to go with the times' and 'to realise that what was good enough 20 years ago will not do for today'.

He deplored the undue attention being given to the pianoforte. 'The different schools of music undoubtedly do wonders as regards musically educating the masses, but I think the harm they do in turning out hundreds of third-rate pianists is incalculable' he told the *Musical Herald*. 'What is wanted to check the veritable avalanche of pianists who threaten us is a school which will *refuse* to take pianoforte students unless they show unmistakable signs of talent.' A young man who came to the School for piano lessons early on in his regime may not have had the level of talent he looked for, but the pianist's subsequent career in a new branch of the entertainment industry would have been approved by one who encouraged his pupils to 'go with the times'. This was Arthur Jarratt who attended the School while a cinema pianist in Peckham. After the 1914 war he became a London cinema manager, and by 1946, when he was

67

knighted, he was managing director of the British Lion Film Corporation.

Landon Ronald was not prepared to recommend that the Music Committee implement the course of action he had outlined to the *Musical Herald*. Early on he realised that Common Councilmen of the City of London were not to be rushed. In fact he hated and dreaded those early committee meetings, but looking back on it all in 1922 he praised John Pakeman as a man of tact and kindness who poured oil on troubled waters and gave him full support.

It was this support which will have emboldened him to propose, as early as 19 December, some six weeks only after his appointment, that the School should shift from its mainly amateur status and enter into competition with the RAM and RCM. He proposed, and the Committee agreed, that the School should be divided into two sections, amateur and professional, with two prospectuses. Amateurs could still come to John Carpenter Street for a few lessons and leave; but those with professional aspirations would be compelled to take two lessons a week in a principal study, one in a secondary study, to learn the rudiments of harmony and attend an orchestral or an operatic class. 'A thorough musical education with the best masters at the least possible fees is my object.' Lionel Tertis was one of the viola teachers; Samuel Taylor Coleridge, the West African composer of *Hiawatha*, was one of his sub-conductors who helped train the student orchestra and chorus, and taught composition. Ronald started new classes—for German lieder and diction, and for French chansons and diction. In their early terms operatic classes were made to start with Sullivan and Flotow and work up to more difficult music. He converted the existing three orchestras into one big band. 'The amateur side will be my special care; and the professional almost my recreation.' With the aid of Henry Saxe Wyndham he introduced a fixed curriculum which up to then had not existed—the School's first definite, systematic course of training for every branch of musical and dramatic education.

His reforms were not confined to educational aspects. He was dismayed that 'most professors appeared to be only on bowing terms with one another, and there was no place where they could foregather or have a meal in comfort.' He found too a pitiful lack of comradeship among the students; nobody seemed to have the smallest interest in anybody else's work. His proudest achievement was founding the

Guildhall School of Music Professors' Club. He won the Music Committee's consent to take over a suite of rooms in the building, furnish them and hand them over to the teaching staff on condition that they formed themselves into a properly constituted club with an annual subscription. 'The entire staff took up the idea with an enthusiasm impossible to describe' he wrote in 1922. The new *bonne camaraderie* had an amazing effect on the work. 'We progressed artistically by leaps and bounds, and it was not very long before those in the know felt that a new and great force was at work in the school. And that force can be described in one word—Unity.'

He would have liked to have seen, too, a properly constituted board which young people could appear before and be advised, without prejudice, whether they should spend money on their musical education with a view to becoming professionals. He pointed out that in singing, the voice was only part of the necessary equipment. Very often ugly girls had fine voices, and vice versa; those with fine singing organs frequently had no musical temperament, no charm, no natural talent for music. Professors were sometimes given to exaggerating the gifts of their pupils, and were responsible for a great deal of money being wasted and many hopes crushed. An independent board could be more objective . . . but what musician is 'objective' in his musical judgements?

His manner and life-style were in direct contrast to William Cummings. He always dressed immaculately, was driven every day to John Carpenter Street in his Rolls Royce and carried himself with the air of being a celebrity, though without ever losing the human touch. Moreover he was a splendid organiser and manager of men. The students adored him. After the last performance of *Yeoman of the Guard* in July 1911 the opera class presented him with a baton 'as a token of esteem and affection'. When Oscar Hammerstein built the London Opera House in Kingsway and opened it in November 1911 as 'opera at theatre prices', the American impresario invited students of the Guildhall School to come and see his productions free of charge by acting as programme sellers. The idea had been a great success at Philadelphia, and unofficially Landon Ronald gave it his blessing. But he had failed to reckon with the strength of the revulsion of English Mothers to anything connected with Theatre. 'I refuse absolutely' a fond parent was quoted as saying, 'to allow my daughter either to sell or to distribute programmes in any theatre whatsoever. . . . I would as soon see her acting in the capacity of a barmaid.' The outcry forced the Principal to issue a statement denying that the idea had ever been contemplated, and Hammerstein's gesture had to be repudiated. The incident drew from *The Bystander* the comment that

> In England we have made music far too genteel. With our bourgeois academies and respectable students, and general atmosphere of chaperoned mediocrity, we deliberately encourage music as an accomplishment for the weaker brethren to the detriment of the true artist who must certainly be independent and probably unconventional.

Such words will have reflected Ronald's sentiments—and maybe were written by him! He was one of 12 sponsors of a scheme to buy Hammerstein's Opera House by public subscription, after the public failed to give the American support, and convert it into the National Opera House at theatre prices but nothing came of this. Richard D'Oyly Carte's earlier English Opera House in Cambridge Circus also failed and was sold to become the home of Variety as the Palace Theatre (still there).

Ronald passed the handling of the 'Public Scandal' (*Daily Express*) surrounding the School's alleged replacement of its English pianos by instruments of German make, to the capable Sir John Pakeman who denounced it as a *canard*. The facts were, he said, that the School hired 50 pianos and under a new arrangement they would have 40 British pianos and 30 German of which ten were being given as gifts. The changeover would take place gradually, he said. In the event, the Music Committee had to bow to the storm and agree not to increase the number of foreign pianos at the School beyond the 27 already contracted for.

At his first prize-giving in November 1911 Ronald asserted that his new plan for dividing the School into an amateur side and a professional side was 'epoch-making'. A hundred students had opted for the professional Prospectus. He was specialising in light opera. Fewer students were now leaving to go elsewhere; the School was catering for what the majority needed. The success of students such as Charles Crabbe, Marie Dare and Henry Geehl, of violinists Margaret Fairless and Boris Pecker, and singers Gladys Ancrum, Dora Labbette and Frederick Blamey demonstrated the wide range of talent which the School now fostered.

His influence in the world of music outside the School made itself felt when, at his instigation, Dame Nellie Melba agreed to found a singing scholarship. He persuaded her to read a paper on 'Singing in English' at the reception held to mark the School's appreciation of her generosity; she wrote the lecture out word by word and rehearsed reading it with her one-time accompanist. The Principal later recollected that she was 'cruelly nervous' when she came to face the crowd of young people in the School theatre that afternoon of 19 May 1911, and after the opening phrases

> with a pathetic smile and a gesture of regret she turned to the audience and said 'I am awfully sorry but I can't go on'. I took the manuscript from her hands and read the paper for her, and was particularly amused the same evening to see in big letters on one of the evening paper placards 'Melba Breaks Down'. Part of her advice was to learn Shelley's *Ode To A Skylark* by heart 'and many other of the poetic ecstasies with which our language is so rich' and speak it out loud 'with distinctness and understanding'.

His enterprising interest in the potential for Music of the new medium of silent moving pictures was reflected in his willingness to conduct the New Symphony Orchestra playing the score written to accompany the film of *The Life of Richard Wagner* made by the Gaumont Company for the Wagner Centenary of 1913 and shown by them at the West End Cinema Theatre in Coventry Street. Wagner was his favourite composer.

With the Professors Club successfully launched at the beginning of 1912, the spirit of unity was extended with the foundation on 18 April of a Students Union. The improvement of Britain's railway system made travel to London from the provinces very much easier and a large proportion of the students were strangers to the metropolis and its vast population. At least one girl in 1912 came up once a week for elocution lessons from Sheffield. The idea of a union had been put forward originally by Orlando Morgan, who formulated the general lines on which it should be run, with both social and educational objectives for past and present studies. Guy Baker was the first honorary secretary, Jenny Hyman its treasurer and Landon Ronald its president. At the end of the Michaelmas Term they produced the first number of *The Magazine of the Guildhall School Musical Union*. In his opening editorial, the anonymous editor said it would seem that nothing was lacking to place the Guildhall School on a footing of absolute equality with the most famous foreign conservatoires. It had not only turned out first-class musicians but been instrumental in diffusing musical knowledge over a continually increasing area. The production of geniuses depended entirely on the supply of raw material available. But the provision of a good musical education, the evocation of a general taste and feeling for things musical depended not only on tuition but also on the creation of an 'atmosphere'. The expansion of a student's ideas and the evocation of his sympathies—human intercourse—was as indispensable as any quality he might bring to it. An educational establishment should aim to foster the gregariousness it created, and the continuation and renewal of old friendships.

The Union held Social Evenings at which ex-students performed—Jenny Hyman at the piano, Max Mossel on the violin. When Joseph Ivimey conducted an orchestra for Blagrove's *Toy Symphony*, Carrie Tubb sang, Albert Sammons played the violin, Sims Reeves the rattle, Orlando Morgan the trumpet and Harriet Sasse was the Nightingale.

But times and tastes were changing; a very less genteel form of music was now being played on occasions less refined than Social Evenings like these. Would Ragtime last? a reporter asked Landon Ronald in April 1913. Was it a serious menace to 'real' music? 'Of course not,' answered the Principal of the Guildhall School of Music. 'It's an amusement, that's all, and it will have the same fate that "Ta-ra-ra-boom-de-ay" met with a few years ago. Take it seriously? Of course not. How could I? Do I dislike it? Not any more than musical comedy. As a matter of fact, I think I prefer ragtime to musical comedy.'

Thoughts were still being given on how best to reduce or eliminate the Corporation's annual subsidy. At a banquet in December 1913 given by Gilbert Wild, chairman of the Music Committee, Harry Bird referred to the possibility of the School obtaining a royal charter. 'The realisation of this honour' he said, 'would give the School a status worthy of the new prestige it has won during recent years, and the great relief in rating expenses would further open up the possibilities of the School.' But with the outbreak of war on 4 August 1914, this, along with a great number of more important things, was lost sight of. The battle of the Steinways and Bechsteins had been fought and lost just in time.

Lilian Stiles-Allen who was to win fame as a soprano is the central figure in this student production of Gluck's *Iphigenia In Tauris*.

The Mikado 1921

If English manufacturers considered that an English name on a piano was a mark of superiority, it was not an attitude shared by musicians who hoped that lack of talent could be obscured by assumption of a more romantic Gypsy or Viennese appellation. When overnight the real citizens of Austria and Hungary, along with those of Germany, became the King's Enemies, the pseudo-Schnitzlers and Aramanyis quickly reverted to Stephens and Atkins. The protection of native performers with English names became the responsibility of the Committee for Music in Wartime (later merged with the Professional Classes War Relief Council), of which the Principal of the Guildhall School of Music was a member, along with H. Walford Davies and R. Vaughan Williams. Ensuring that music was not a casualty in circumstances which would seem to claim more urgent priorities, was their aim. 'We are in the midst of a terrible, dastardly war thrust on us by an unscrupulous enemy' wrote Landon Ronald in October 1914. 'Let it be remembered that the musician, both successful and unsuccessful, is among the acute sufferers.' 'It goes without saying' stated Ernest Newman in the *Musical Times* in a leader headed 'The War and the Future of Music', that

> art of every kind will be profoundly affected by the intellectual outcome of all these changes, and music perhaps more than the other arts.... For purely economic reasons the whole business of music performing and music publishing is bound to suffer for years to come.... Musicians may well doubt the sanity of a world in which Kreisler is in arms against Ysaÿe and Thibaud, in which it is the business of those of us who owe some of the finest moments of our life to the great living German composers to do all we can to prevent their pouring out any more of their genius on us.

Where should the Guildhall School of Music, with its many 'enemy' staff, stand in all this? In January, for instance, they had just appointed Liza Lehmann as a Professor of Singing. Landon Ronald's relations with the Corporation must have been strained as never before when he found it politic to have to agree to their issuing the announcement of 15 August. 'The Music Committee of the Corporation of London' this said, 'have decided to dispense with the services of all German, Austrian and Hungarian professors at the Guildhall School of Music. From this date only pianos of British make will be used in the School.' *Musical News* said the decision would be received with mixed feelings; it hoped that naturalised

Britons would be treated as native-born Britons. At John Carpenter Street the rule would apply to Olga Neruda, George Muller, Paul Stoeving, Hans Brousil, Alfred Kastner and Kalman Ronay. Are they responsible for the madness of the Kaiser? asked the *Musical Herald* which took the same stance as *Musical News*, 'or for the brutes who have desolated Belgium?' Anti-German feeling was intensified in May 1915 when a U-boat sunk the SS *Lusitania*. One of the 760 survivors was the Welsh tenor Parry Jones who was to become a teacher at the Guildhall School.

Landon Ronald agreed to do without German music in the concerts which he and Sir Thomas Beecham were giving in the Albert Hall but confessed, when it was all over, that now and then his soul had cried out for Beethoven and Brahms.

Inevitably the number of students attending the Guildhall School fell away, but there was no question of closing down, though many asked why 'waste' money on Music Training at such a time of crisis? 'What do you think they would say' was the Principal's spirited reply,

> if, when they return, they find everything disbanded and broken up because we chose to consider it unpatriotic to run such things in wartime? There are thousands of our students serving at the front who trust us to keep the flag flying and who are longing to return to us to resume the various studies they loved so well. Isn't it our sacred duty to see they are not disappointed?

A few carping critics had held the view, when hostilities had broken out, that anything not having a direct bearing on the war should be abandoned.

> But the Guildhall School of Music has gone on with its good work with greater enthusiasm and greater artistic success than ever, as is proved by the wonderful manner in which the number of students have kept up the quality of the work done. (1917)

In London and the provinces Light Opera flourished more than ever, and the Guildhall School continued to turn out worthy recruits. The conductor Herman Darewski gave a scholarship for aspirants for light opera and grand opera. Sydney Baynes, composer of the 'Destiny Waltz' which brought much romance to the drabness of wartime Britain, learnt his craft at the Guildhall School. When 19-year old Dorothy Waring, who had won the Melba scholarship, left the School in 1915 she was at once engaged by George Edwardes as leading lady in his production of Messager's *Véronique* on a three-year contract. The star pupil of the wartime concert platform and opera stage was Lilian Stiles-Allen.

All competitions were kept up, and in 1915 Henry Ainley came and judged the entrants for the Elocution prizes. A distinguished drama student of the wartime period was Edna Best whose partnership with Herbert Marshall was a bright feature of the theatre of the twenties and thirties. In July 1916 she played Puck in the student production of *A Stratford Pageant 1616–1916* written by May Shepperd and Henry Saxe Wyndham for the School's Shakespeare Tercentenary celebrations.

News of such continued enterprise comforted the last years of William Cummings who died on 10 June 1915 aged 83, a link with a world of which, thanks to the accelerated changes brought by the 'Great War', there was no longer any trace. Born before Queen Victoria came to the throne, as a boy alto in the front row of a choir singing *Elijah* conducted by the composer, he had been praised for his singing by Felix Mendelssohn who had patted him on his head and asked his name. He left behind a marvellous musician's working library: like the Novello library earlier, it was offered to the School but it was decided there was insufficient money to maintain it. So such autographs as Purcell's *Dido and Aeneas* (now priceless) went to the saleroom—and the School had to wait another 60 years for a respectable library.

Students of the Guildhall School played their part in 'war work' by forming concert parties to entertain soldiers at hospitals. An appeal was made through the *Union Magazine* for people to make up a quartet, for a Reciter and a Good Accompanist. Each member of the party, said the note, must be 'decidedly capable' and used to performing in public. Many of the wounded in hospitals were frequently tormented by incompetent amateur performers. 'It is quite unfair that hospital patients who have no means of retaliating should be subjected to so many laryngeal experiments.'

With the Armistice of November 1918 and the Peace of 1919 there came no quick return to normal. Colonial soldiers, and demobilised British servicemen and nurses, were accepted at the Guildhall School under the Army Education Scheme. A Sub-Committee of the Music Committee considered the question of accepting German and Austrian students again, but after adjourning for three months in

October 1919, and then for another six months, on 23 April 1920 the minutes recorded 'reference discharged'.

The School gradually got back into its peacetime stride. At the beginning of the academic year 1917 there had been only 1,423 students. By the end of the Summer term in 1921, numbers were up to 2,882. This was a peak and thereafter the figures slowly declined again. The cost of living rose as a result of the war, and the Special Sub-Committee once more considered applying for the royal Charter which would reduce its rates, but thought better of it. When its rival which already had one, the Royal Academy of Music, and had moved to its present site in Marylebone Road in 1912, celebrated its centenary in 1922, the Music Committee offered its congratulations and presented it with an engraved address signed by the Lord Mayor, the Chairman of the Committee, the Principal and Secretary. It was the year in which Landon Ronald was knighted, not particularly for his work as Principal of the Guildhall School but for his contribution to Music, his eminence as a composer and conductor—and a reward for the musical instruction he had been giving over the years to Queen Alexandra. It was good for the prestige of the City's music school, and staff and students were delighted.

In the first volume of reminiscences *Variations On A Personal Theme* (Chapter 21, 'Speaking Seriously') which Sir Landon had published in 1922, he confessed to having promised the Music Committee not to stay more than three years, yet there he still was after 11. A *bon viveur* lionised by Society, he was not physically strong, and his insistence on travelling all over Britain to conduct hundreds of concerts every year, composing songs, making gramophone records, fulfilling his obligations as Musical Adviser to The Gramophone Company (he started a Gramophone Club at the School in 1929), to say nothing of writing his memoirs, as well as directing the fortunes of the Guildhall School, played havoc with his health and, on his own admission, he suffered all the while from rheumatism, lumbago, sciatica and indigestion. But there were always new challenges which demanded his attention.

1922 saw the dawning of a new source of employment for the talents of those who left the School with professional ambitions. In May that year manufacturers of receiving sets and components held a Conference on Wireless Telephony Broadcasting which led to the formation on 18 October of a British Broadcasting Company to transmit music and speech to all able to receive it in the headphones of their mysterious crystal sets and the horned loudspeakers connected to the more powerful receivers with the valves they called bright emitters. Twenty-two-year old Clemence Bradley of Folkestone, who was a singing pupil of Albert Garcia at the Guildhall School, took part in the first concert broadcast by the BBC from its 2LO studio on the seventh floor of Marconi House in the Strand.* This led to the BBC broadcasting an entire Guildhall School of Music concert on 11 July 1923. A student who acquired national fame through the wireless in 1925 was Albert Sandler who won a scholarship after playing his violin in a cinema orchestra in those pre-talkie days. In 1922, at 16, he joined the Lyons Corner House Orchestra and graduated to the Trocadero Restaurant in Shaftesbury Avenue as star violinist. He was later to be remembered for his 'Grand Hotel' programme which the BBC introduced in 1941. Violin student William Primrose was only 19 when he made his debut at the Queen's Hall in 1923, and became principal viola player in Toscanini's National Broadcasting Orchestra in the US. Oscar Rabin won a Guildhall School scholarship at the age of 12 and two years later was playing professionally in radio bands before starting his own career as a bandleader. Henry Hall, who went to the BBC to direct their dance band in 1932 after 11 years in charge of the music at the hotels of the London, Midland and Scottish Railway, was a student in 1922. Singer Gwen Catley and actress Barbara Couper who were students in the 1920s made new names for themselves on the wireless, though of course both had already established reputations outside the studios. A contemporary of theirs at the School was Sidney Harrison who returned as a professor in 1927. A conductor and concert pianist who was to tour the world, he is still an enthusiastic broadcaster who not only gives recitals but has a world-wide reputation for his illustrated talks on Music. In the thirties he gave the first television piano lesson. Maurice Cole and Raymond Newell were other students of this time who reached vast audiences through the new medium of sound broadcasting which, it seemed, should bring the social and educative benefits which William Cummings thought would come from Music

* In July 1920 the voice of Dame Nellie Melba had been transmitted by 'wireless telephone' to the Applied Electricity Laboratory of Liverpool University from the Marconi Works at Chelmsford.

being taken to 'the masses'. To what extent those hopes were fulfilled it is impossible to say, but certainly the general public in the twenties were made aware of the existence and work of the Guildhall School of Music as never before, by the regular Sunday afternoon broadcasts from the concert hall at John Carpenter Street of the Church Cantatas of Bach, 'with the tones of your organ' as Sir John Reith remarked, 'blending with our instruments and voices'. Despite the Music Committee's intentions, they could not afford an organ in the concert hall when it was built, but an Organ Fund had been started and one was purchased from Norman, Hill and Beard in 1907, with three manuals and a patent kinetic blower. (It was still in the derelict Blackfriars School in 1980.)

There were innovations in other fields. A class for the study of Dalcroze Eurythmics was started, and a Students Repertory Theatre formed. In 1923, to commemorate his membership of the Corporation, F. D. Bowles JP generously put at the disposal of the Music Committee sufficient stock to produce an income for the foundation of a Students Endowment Fund. Two who came to the School to study the piano under Orlando Morgan at this time who will not have had occasion to call on this fund in later life were certainly Nöel Coward and Fred Astaire. Nöel Coward was to record: 'The short period I spent at the Guildhall School was a very happy one, and I thoroughly enjoyed myself there. If I had had more time I would have taken a longer course.' As he disagreed with most of the harmony his teacher tried to get him to write—'why can't I write consecutive fifths if I want to?'—his stay might not in any case have been too long; but it was a genuine renewal of friendship when Coward accepted the Fellowship of the School, presented on the School's behalf by another Fellow and friend Bernard (now Lord) Miles, in 1972.

A stage comedian, whose success in musical comedy and revue followed his appearances in 'Footlights' shows at Cambridge, expanded his audience in the same way as Fred Astaire was to do—through the other new medium which offered employment to students: talking pictures. This was Jack Hulbert who was not only himself a student at the School; his father Dr Henry Hulbert was a lecturer there on Voice and Elocution.

In 1924 Sir Landon Ronald created a Conducting Class to which he appointed as professor Julius Harrison, conductor of the British

from Sir Edward Elgar, Master of the King's Music; from Sir Arthur Pinero whose *Trelawney of the Wells* had just been given in the School theatre; from Sir Granville Bantock, Director of the Birmingham and Midlands Institute School of Music—there had been an Instruction in Singing class at the Institute since 1859; and from ex-students of the younger generation who were making their mark such as Nöel Coward. Sybil Thorndike said she had worked and made her career in another branch of Art from that which she had studied at the School,

> but I say without hesitation that it is to my years there and the influence which was over me then that I owe the ideals of work which I have tried to follow during my career in the theatre. Such a background, such a foundation, must be of great value to any artist, and I feel when one is continually brought in conflict with the lesser ideals of commercial success it is immensely refreshing to one's soul to remember one's student days and the maxims that were continually driven into one, that nothing counts but sincere, careful study, and ceaseless and relentless application to the job in hand. For this I am grateful to my professors— Madame Bessie Cox, Dr Arthur Greenish, and my well-loved pianoforte teacher, Francesco Berger—and the happy years spent working at the Guildhall School of Music.

R. D. Blumenfeld, editor-in-chief of the *Daily Express*, said that the School, which might be called either a conservatory or a musical forge, had progressed far beyond the hopes, aspirations and enthusiasms of its founders; and he was convinced that the rare combination of genius, personality, pluck, industry and humanity which characterised its 57-year old *maestro* had made possible that happy consummation. He had never seen Sir Landon at work, but he had seen him at play—'and you may take it from me that if he plays at the piano as well as he plays at playing he is indeed a genius.'

> I shall probably be induced to alter my estimate of my friend if I had occasion to observe him at his daily task, but this is a treat which has never been vouchsafed to me. The only personal experience I have of the Guildhall School of Music is that I pass its doors occasionally on my way to and from Fleet Street, and then my ears are assailed by a discordant jumble of tonic sol fas, tenori robustos, high sopranos and rhapsodical piano echoes and I always say to myself: 'There's Landon at work at last!' Anyhow it shows that the thing is a going concern, which means a lot in these depressing days. . . . Sir Landon is to me something far more valuable than the mere captain of his craft, more worth

knowing than just the deservedly great magician who wangles beautiful tones with a baton out of a hundred men with instruments in their hands, and that is the Landon Ronald whom I know and have always loved; just the simple, honest, clean-thinking man of the world, with poetry in his soul and music in his heart, on whom one can lean heavily as a friend and find him standing the strain with a smile on his face. I know, for I have tried him and he has never flinched from the ordeal.

The object of this adulation was himself writing his second volume of memoirs in this jubilee year. The very fact that he had passed 21 of the best years of his life directing the fortunes of the Guildhall School must surely speak for itself, he mused. The Corporation of London would not have put up with him all that time if he had been a failure, and he certainly would not have stood it for 21 *days* had he not loved the work and been surrounded by a loyal and affectionate professional staff, and had the assistance of his friend Henry Saxe Wyndham the Secretary.

> I have many valued friends among the Corporation, and I have found those who come into actual contact with the working of the School are always enthusiastic and proud of it. I venture to think however there are one or two points in the management of the School by the Corporation which call for attention or at least should be seriously modified.
>
> (*Myself and Others, Written Lest I Forget*, 1931)

But that was not the place to discuss such matters, he said. His reward for the work and energy he had expended on the School had been, firstly, appreciation and the friendship shown to him by the Chairman, Sir John Pakeman, and other members of the Music Committee; secondly, the exceptional number of talented young students who had made good before the public and become successful artists; and thirdly, the splendid work accomplished by the professors. 'I have been well loved and well served, and no man can ask for more.'

The 'depressing days' deplored by R. D. Blumenfeld were the product of the Economic Crisis which now engulfed not only Britain, where there were soon to be more than two million unemployed, but the whole world. The number of students dropped once more—to 1,628 by 1930, when new entrants numbered a mere 153. Sir Landon regretfully had to cancel the School's production of *Véronique* and a concert at Queens Hall, but enlisted Carrie Tubb as a Professor of Singing, which surely attracted embryo prima donnas.

The goodwill and publicity generated by the Jubilee celebrations had been incalculable. Principal, Secretary, students and teachers now settled down to build on it and face with renewed confidence whatever the future might bring. As Edna Best said in her Souvenir Booklet message,

> It is pleasing to think that though governments may fall, great personalities cease to be, the Guildhall School will still go on, it being an essential part of the basis of one of the greatest of the arts.

PART TWO

The ancient custom of this honourable and renowned Citie hath been ever to retaine and maintaine excellent and expert Musicians.

Thomas Morley (1599)

Don't put your daughter on the stage, Mrs Worthington.

Ex-Guildhall School student, N. Coward (1935)

Edric Cundell
The fifth Principal of the Guildhall School
1938–1959

5 Edric Cundell's 'School of Mozart'

Little changed at John Carpenter Street during the nineteen-thirties. Though built for the young people of an age long past, the place had an air about it which endeared it to all who used it. The glass windows in the double doors of the individual classrooms had become the medium for the exchange of cheery signals between the occupants and passers-by, rather than peep-holes through which the guardians of student morals could assure themselves (and worried parents) that what was going on was instruction and not hanky-panky. Dress had changed and hairstyles—less formal, but not too casual. After all this was London, not 'the provinces'. Seniors were expected to set an example by wearing a suit. When bass singer Norman Walker appeared in the School one day in grey flannel trousers and a tweed sports jacket, the Principal called him into his office and reminded him that as the holder of a major scholarship he must never come again in 'week-end' attire. If he did not know where to go for a suit in London at a price within his means, he recommended The Fifty Shilling Tailors in the Strand.

But as Max Morgan, who became a student at the School in September 1930, recollected 50 years later, although Sir Landon Ronald may have had notions about behaviour and appearance which not all could share, his personality and authority as a musician had an electrifying effect if, for instance, he should happen to put his head round the door of the concert hall during a rehearsal and stop to listen. 'When on a rare occasion he took the baton, we became completely different human beings.'

Late Victorian and Edwardian elegance had passed, but in 1932 the Head Porter still wore a top hat and made great ceremony of opening the door of the Rolls Royce in which the Principal arrived each day from his house in Warwick Avenue and wishing him good morning. There was always a log fire in the front hall in wintertime, and any student who was warming himself beside it at the moment of Sir

Landon's entrance was well advised to make as quick an exit as possible.

Arthur Reckless, who won a scholarship on the strength of demonstrating his fine baritone voice to the Principal, was assigned to the School's most distinguished teacher, Walter Hyde. While still a student he made a gramophone record of Coleridge Taylor songs for HMV and by 1934 had begun singing on the BBC. (Empire Service transmissions were live, and he often had to be in good voice at 3 a.m.) At the end of his last term Sir Landon asked him to come and see him in his office. It was not to be reprimanded for any dread social misdemeanour, but to be invited to join the staff. In January 1937, Reckless became the youngest professor of singing the Guildhall School of Music had ever had—and in 1980 he was still at it.

A serious drama student befriended by Arthur Reckless in the 1930s was Cyril Fletcher, another whose stage reputation as a comedian became a national one thanks to the wireless. A pupil of Kate Rorke and Frank Ridley, he distinguished himself in straight roles such as Antonio in Robert Atkins's producton of *The Merchant of Venice* and Cranmer in Bax's *The Rose Without A Thorn*. His success in the Fol-de-Rols concert party at Hastings set the pattern of his future career; it was in one of their shows that he recited 'Dreamin' of Thee', which fathered all the odd odes to come. With Nelson Keys, Douglas Byng and Valerie Hobson he was a pioneer of television revue.

In the cast of the Clifford Bax play with Cyril Fletcher was Donald Bissett, who took part in the performance by the Dramatic Class of John Van Druten's *London Wall* along with a man who was to make his name not on the stage but as a writer of spy novels, Eric Ambler. Being taught by Kate Rorke at this time, too, was Diana Churchill. A member of the Junior Comedy Class in *The Red Umbrella* was Peter Cushing, who in 1980 was still frightening audiences in the latest of a long saga of horror films. Training to be a baritone was the Old Etonian brother of Gilbert Frankau the novelist, Ronald Frankau, who was to win fame however not as a concert singer but as a comedian whose quick patter ended with an even quicker comic song.

Other students who gravitated to the music hall after training at the School in the 1930s as serious musicians were Doris Waters, who took piano lessons, and her sister Elsie, who trained to be a violinist. Their first sister act was almost entirely musical, with Elsie playing pieces on

recommending to the Court of Common Council the names of two or three who they were satisfied were suited for the post of Principal, and the nominees duly presented themselves to the Court in full morning dress (cutaway tails, stiff white collar) to give the Councillors a 20-minute address on their qualifications. There was the usual spate of prognostication on the likely choice. Stanley Chapple (conductor of the opera) was widely backed, but the Court opted for a recently-appointed repetiteur at Glyndebourne, 45-year-old Edric Cundell. Cundell had won a piano scholarship at the Trinity College of Music. During the Great War he was in the British Army on the Salonica front, which was quiet enough to allow him to compose a symphonic poem for orchestra which he called 'Serbia', the first performance of which was given by the Royal Guard of King Alexander of Serbia. He was awarded the Order of the Serbian White Eagle for his military exploits. After the war he was appointed an examiner at Trinity College and played the horn in the orchestra of Covent Garden opera house. At Glyndebourne under Fritz Busch he gained a lasting admiration for, and working knowledge of, that great musical director's productions of the operas of Mozart. He had also worked there with singers from the School such as Joyce Newton and Norman Walker. It was his enterprising reproduction of many Mozart operas *à la* Glyndebourne with student casts at the Guildhall School which made his regime contrast musically so strongly with that of the Sir Landon Ronald era of Gilbert and Sullivan, Flotow and Messager. He was altogether a very different character from his predecessor, informal, modest and very approachable. In his first public address, he announced he was instituting a second Opera Class for the study of 'more musically significant' operas. It was no surprise therefore that the first opera performed under Edric Cundell's personal direction—February 1939—was Mozart's *Così Fan Tutte* with the same Rose Hill as Fiordiligi and the Principal conducting every performance. When Owen Brannigan sang in the second opera production, Offenbach's *La Vie Parisienne* in May, Stanley Chapple conducted ... the runner-up for Principal evidently bore no hard feelings.

Cundell had his two opera classes running in parallel. He also extended the studies of drama students to designing and making costumes and scenery. More significantly still he planned to install a broadcasting studio for instruction in microphone technique which would also be fitted with equipment for the practical study of Television and Stagecraft—the BBC had made the world's first public transmissions of television in 1936.

It was an enterprising decision, but unhappily an ill-timed one. For within months of his announcement all television transmissions were closed 'for the duration'. The summer of 1939 ended with a concert on 14 July in which the student orchestra played Mozart's 34th Symphony and Brahms' Variations on a Theme by Haydn, and with a Dancing and Dramatic Recital on 18 July, the School's 2,160th performance. The programmes carried the note: 'The Autumn Term begins on Monday, 18th September 1939'.

So the School had two weeks of its summer vacation still to run when war was declared on 3 September. Waddington the Secretary was for postponing the start of the new term, if not keeping the School closed indefinitely. But the new Principal wrote to the Music Committee saying in his opinion 'every effort ought to be made to keep the School open'. In anticipation of immediate air attacks, the Committee thought better of assembling so many young people in one place in the likely target area of the City of London, but when the raids failed to materialise they decided to re-open the School on 2 October on condition that no more than 50 people were allowed in the building at any one time. The air raid shelter was enlarged to take 100, and on 4 December, at Cundell's suggestion, the Committee, under its new chairman H. Roper Barrett, agreed to that number attending. They accepted Cundell's recommendation that the School should remain open in the evenings, that £45 should be spent on blackout material, that they should open next term on 1 January 1940, and thenceforward carry on 'in a normal manner as circumstances permit, all special restrictions as to times of attendance and number of students being removed'.

The first concert of the war was held on 29 November 1939 in which Walter Hyde's pupils Rose Hill and Llewellyn John sang 'By all that we hold sacred' from *Don Giovanni.* Publication of the Student Magazine was suspended, and meetings of the Union stopped. Wartime travelling restrictions prevented many students from hazarding the train journey to London from the provinces; most parents of overseas students called their sons and daughters home without further delay. All students and staff who were physically fit and of military age soon became involved in the Call-up, and were reporting to units of the Navy, Army and Air Force in various parts of Britain and overseas. Student singer David Lloyd, for instance, joined the Welsh Guards (with whose band he was able to make a number of recordings); Charles Henden, who had become a member of the staff in the Registration Office in 1935 and was already in the Territorial Army, was commissioned into the Essex Regiment and seconded to the African Rifles.

Arthur Reckless was commissioned into the Royal Air Force, but not before he had taken part in the Longest Prom on Record. This was in the Queen's Hall where, on the sounding of the air-raid siren, the concert ground to a halt and the manager told the audience that he had been advised that no one should leave the building. So they stayed—until three the next morning. After the rehearsed programme, Arthur Reckless and his fellow-soloist Eva Turner ran through their entire repertoire; Sir Henry Wood conducted emotional community singing. Miss Turner (now Dame Eva and still a great friend of the School) remembers the tears in her eyes. Volunteers were invited to do their party pieces, and a man in the balcony stood up and yodelled.

Edric Cundell went ahead with his plans for the Opera Class to stage Osmond Raphael's production of Mozart's *Don Giovanni* in the second week of July 1940 but had to cancel them. There was no longer the talent or the numbers. He kept the School open for the summer vacation however, and the new Lady Superintendent, Marjorie Browne, saw that the few students able to attend had every amenity. In September the Music Committee decided to open again for half a term only—until 28 October—and then consider suspending activities altogether. On 29 October they cautiously opted for continuing until 7 December and then to review the situation once more. On that date they decided to carry on so long as there were students willing to take the risk. A note was printed on every concert and play programme:

> If an air raid warning is sounded, it will be reinforced by the continuous ringing of the Hall Bell (as distinct from the intermittent ringing marking the end of any intervals during performances).

The performance would continue until the Lady Superintendent reported imminent danger, but anyone wishing to take shelter at once should feel no hesitation in doing so when the curtain was lowered for that purpose. Accommodation in the School Shelter was limited and admission was regulated by the issue of white discs handed to those entering the School by the hall porter.

Local examinations were held as usual but of course the whole scale of the operation both in London and the provinces was greatly reduced. There had been 1,183 students and 124 new entrants for the summer term of 1939, the last before the War (Mark 2). Only 332 presented themselves for the autumn term, with 48 new students. By the autumn term of 1940 there were only 216, the lowest attendance figure since 1880.

No student or teacher suffered when damage was done to the School during the 'intense and indiscriminate attack' with high explosives and incendiaries by German bombers on Saturday night 10 May 1941 when five hospitals, Westminster Abbey, the British Museum and the House of Commons were hit, the roof of Westminster Hall pierced and the face of Big Ben scarred. At Victoria Embankment the ceiling on the underside of the gallery in the School theatre collapsed; the upholstery of the seats was ruined by dirt and water; the lift was made inoperable, and all the pictures lent by the Guildhall Art Gallery destroyed. Busts of Dr Cummings and Sir Landon Ronald had been removed to safe custody in the country. The building by the Thames had had a lucky escape. A main inconvenience was the postponement, until the theatre could be repaired, of the drama students' production of Esther McCracken's long-running comedy *Quiet Wedding*.

The School was again kept open for the summer vacation of 1941, by now down to 170 students. The finances of the operation gave the Corporation concern, and the Coal, Corn and Finance Committee conferred with the Music Committee 'to consider the question of the future of the Guildhall School of Music and Drama, and of the staff engaged'. They decided it must continue. In the meantime Edric Cundell's musical talents were in great demand and he conducted orchestras in concerts all over Britain.

Some—mostly businessmen and often refugees—came to the School for training in subjects other than music and drama. Public-speaking classes proved so popular in 1942 that a third exam was introduced between Introductory and Proficiency grades, and the increased number who were ready to pay helped to swell the funds. In 1943 a new Diploma of Honorary Membership was instituted, and the first recipient was the redoubtable ex-chairman Sir John Pakeman; the following year it was awarded to Sir Adrian Boult.

With morale on the home front stimulated by news of Allied successes on the various fronts overseas, people began coming to the School again in greater numbers—1,157 in the autumn term of 1943. Many students were given contracts to entertain audiences of servicemen by the Entertainments National Service Association (ENSA) and the Council for Entertainment, Music and the Arts (CEMA). Ex-student Isidore Godfrey, who had been a gold medallist in Sir Landon Ronald's day and was now musical director of the D'Oyly Carte company, was constantly on tour with Gilbert and Sullivan operas.

In June 1944 the School gladly accepted from Austrians in Britain a bigger-than-life bronze head of Beethoven sculpted by the Austrian Alexander Jaray. By this time, there was very little antipathy towards those from Germany and Austria who had taken refuge in Britain in the late 1930s. The teaching of Max Rostal, the Austrian violinist who had been on the staff of the Guildhall School since coming to Britain in 1934, was in greater demand than ever.

Kate Rorke celebrated her 80th birthday in 1944 and her pupil Diana Churchill organised a testimonial. The famous actress whose activities at John Carpenter Street had led, more than anything else, to the addition of 'and Drama' to the School's name, had only a few months to live; she died in July 1945. When in June 1944 the home of Jenny Hyman who had been a teacher at the School for 34 years was hit by a bomb, ex-students Dame Myra Hess and Irene Scharrer gave a piano recital as a 'Hyman Benefit'. Ill-health forced W. P. Waddington to resign as Secretary that year and he was succeeded by Raymond Rayner, a former student who had performed in Sir Landon Ronald's last opera.

The majority of students had always been female, even in peacetime, and naturally their preponderance was now greater than ever. Among those whose studies in the somewhat bleak circumstances of the wartime Guildhall School of Music and Drama started them on noteworthy professional careers were opera singer Olwen Davies who married fellow student Leslie Murchie, and actress Honor Blackman who appeared in one of the last student plays of the war, James Barrie's *Dear Brutus*, produced by Maurice Browning. In the very last play production before peace came, Dodie Smith's *Dear*

Octopus produced by Raymond Rayner, was a student actress whose future career had by 1980 made her one of the most familiar faces in television situation comedy, Mollie Sugden.

At the first distribution of prizes after the war ended in 1945 Edric Cundell was able to announce that the School now had 1,500 students with a waiting list of 200. They were the best figures since 1924. The numbers—and income—had been swelled by 50 American servicemen who, from September 1945, paid for a specially designed 12-week music refresher course, and more if they wished to take drama. These were 'GIs' who had started music or drama in the United States before being drafted into the 'General Intake', and were awaiting being sent home for demobilisation. They were fascinated by the Victorian atmosphere of the place, the dusty, dark corridors and the antiquated 'elevator'. They had nothing like that in Dallas or San Francisco. Their presence—and enthusiasm—were stimulating to the teaching staff. 'It keeps you on your toes' owned one professor, 'when you've a man in your class who was 12 years with the New York Theatre Guild.'

The traffic across the Atlantic was of course two-way. A wartime 'evacuee' in the USA was Claire Bloom who became a drama student at the Guildhall School on return to England and at 16 was given a film contract by J. Arthur Rank. She played Ophelia in the 1948 Shakespeare Festival production of *Hamlet* at Stratford-on-Avon and returned to receive the Diploma of Fellowship in 1974. Demobbed British servicemen took advantage of the Labour Government's post-war Further Educational Grants Scheme to obtain an inexpensive musical education from the best teachers. They raised the intake, but many were casual rather than serious students of music. Max Morgan and Cimbro Martin helped senior students teach music to a hundred children aged nine and upwards who were selected from the southern counties for the musical promise they had already shown, and came to the Guildhall School every Saturday morning under what was known as the Junior Exhibition Scheme sponsored by the various local education authorities. The Junior Music Department was still going strong in 1980, but completely revised under a professional staff, as shown later.

Coming back to John Carpenter Street after six years service in the army abroad, Charles Henden sensed a new vivacity. World War had once more accelerated social change—in behaviour, attitudes, dress.

The trend was for more informality and less reverence, but for years yet 'official' audiences would wear dinner jackets and long evening dresses. They were specially smart of course on 'Court Nights' when the Lord Mayor and the Music Committee were in ritual attendance.

From 1945, in the Concert Hall, 'experimental rehearsals' of the latest compositions were given by young professionals—many of them ex-students—under the auspices of the Committee for the Promotion of New Music (now the SPNM). The BBC re-started its television transmissions which probably curtailed the number of engagements to be had in what was now called 'radio', but opened up a completely new field for professional musicians and actors. In 1945, at the request of the Ministry of Education, the School began giving Graduate Diploma Courses in Music which carried Degree status for teaching purposes in Britain. The shortage of teachers in all subjects was severe immediately after the war, and this was one of the many 'Emergency Training' schemes financed by the Ministry. Unlike many similar courses, however, the 'GGSM' Diploma not only survived this time of emergency but, in 1979, became the first music college diploma to carry 'Honours Degree' status.

The Principal now had the opportunity of mounting the student Mozart productions which he had dreamed about Before The War; and in June 1946 he presented *The Marriage of Figaro* in a style which broke entirely new ground for productions in the School theatre. But when the heir to the throne, the young Princess Elizabeth, and her sister Princess Margaret, decided to honour the School with a visit that November, Edric Cundell thought a more acceptable offering would be Gilbert and Sullivan, and the royal princesses, after being received by the Lord Mayor, Sir Bracewell Smith, were highly entertained by a spirited student production of *Iolanthe*.

One day in 1947 the Principal had to go to Cardiff to conduct a concert for Sir Adrian Boult who had been taken ill. Before he left he told Arthur Reckless he had some applicants for grants coming to see him for voice tests. Would he go to his office at the appropriate time and hear the four young men in his place? Jenny Hyman as usual was the official accompanist, and Arthur Reckless heard each in turn, sitting in the Principal's chair. The last of the four was a handsome young man, a baritone, with a fine voice and immense verve, whose name was Geraint Evans. A member of the Pontypridd Operatic Society before the war, he had been singing on the British Forces

Network of the BBC in Hamburg where he was stationed with his unit as part of the British Army of Occupation. There he had found himself a German professor, Tajo Hermann, who taught him the so-called 'continental' method of breathing. On demob, he won a scholarship from the Covent Garden Opera House which entitled him to further training in Italy and Switzerland. He was thus a veteran student of 26 when he came before Arthur Reckless, the 'stand-in' Principal of the Guildhall School of Music and Drama, in the summer of 1947. Walter Hyde, with whom he wished to study operatic singing, had a full list, so the young Welsh baritone took a course of lessons with one of the School's two German professors, Walther Gruner, who was familiar with the continental breathing method. While still at the Guildhall School, Geraint Evans was taking parts at Covent Garden and poised for the career which was to take him to all the most famous opera houses of the world, and gain him a knighthood (the first to be given to an opera singer before retirement since Edward VII honoured Charles Santley in 1907). In 1950 he sang his first *Messiah* with Heddle Nash and a 20-year old coloratura soprano who had won a scholarship at the Guildhall School, Patricia Varley, who was to become a principal soprano with the Carl Rosa Company.

A contemporary of Geraint Evans, whose career developed in a very different direction, was George Martin who, as head of Parlophone, heard the demonstration record which other companies had dismissed, and decided to invite the Liverpool group who had made it to London for a test, saw their potential and stage-managed the phenomenal success of the Beatles as makers of gramophone records. Even more important he made the musical arrangements for the Beatles and shared the responsibility of developing the Beatles sound.

Martin had taught himself to play the classics on the piano, and after demob from the Fleet Air Arm in 1947 found himself at the age of 21 on the brink of joining the civil service when his talent as a pianist came to the notice of Sidney Harrison, who secured him a place at the Guildhall School. He studied composition and conducting, and took up the oboe. In 1950 he was given a part-time job with EMI, recording classical music directly on to wax with only one sound track. By 1956 he was in full charge of their Parlophone operation, and in that capacity came to handle the Beatles records.

Student of the violin and trombone at about this time was Chris Barber, jazz player and bandleader, who formed his own band at the age of 24 in 1954, the year another Guildhall School student set up an equally famous band, Eric Delaney, who studied timpani, joined Geraldo and became one of the best known jazz drummers in Britain.

Others who attended the School in this period whose careers followed more orthodox lines were singers Peter Glossop, Pauline Tinsley, and Maureen Lehane. Drama students included Michael Jayston, Anthony Newlands, Frederick Jaeger, and Brewster Mason. Edric Cundell carried through his highly praised series of Mozart operas produced in the School theatre by Osmond Raphael, and received a much deserved CBE in 1949.

Winning a second world war had demanded unprecedented sacrifice, but by 1950 Britain was well on the way to economic and industrial recovery. In the process society had changed many of its attitudes. A climate of opinion was forming in which it was no longer quite so 'un-English' to confess to playing the flute or having spent the evening at the opera. Not only in the metropolis, but through its examination representatives in provincial areas all over the United Kingdom, the Guildhall School of Music and Drama had not only survived, but made sure it was here to stay.

After rehearsal, 1950

Up to Room 69, 1950

Gordon Thorne
The sixth Principal of the Guildhall School
1959–1965

6 Music and Drama: Gordon Thorne structures

A hundred years after Prince Albert's Great Exhibition of 1851 Britain mounted another to mark the centenary, as 'one united act of national reassessment and one corporate reaffirmation of faith in the nation's future'. A principal aim of the Festival of Britain 1951 was 'to bring to the British way of life some enrichment that will endure for long after the Festival year is over'. The Arts were displayed in a series of country-wide musical and dramatic performances and exhibitions, but one building of the South Bank Exhibition in London was to remain there permanently—the Royal Festival Hall. It seated 3,300 and had room for an orchestra of more than 100 players and a choir of 250. 'Innovations include the double-skinned wall designed to exclude noise' stated the official Guide, 'and the tuning of the concert hall auditorium after the building work had been completed.' This tuning was undertaken in February 1951 by engineers of the London County Council checking the auditorium for tone and acoustics, while the 86-strong student orchestra of the Guildhall School of Music and Drama played Beethoven's *Coriolan* Overture three times in succession to 3,000 members of the LCC staff sitting on cushions on the floor which had not yet been fitted with seats. The young players paid no attention to the comments which were shouted across their heads—'A bit woolly at the back of the stalls on low frequencies!'— nor to the six revolver shots which rang out half way through. No one had been assassinated. It was just an attendant firing blanks as part of a reverberation test.

That year Edric Cundell was made a member of the new Arts Council which, in the absence of an un-English Ministry of the Arts, the Government had created to handle the taxpayers' money which it was prepared to allocate to the Arts. He was appointed Chairman of its Music Panel. The following year he broke away from Mozart with Verdi's *Falstaff*, produced by Sumner Austin. To give as many students experience as possible, there were two casts. The Principal conducted the orchestra, and in the cast was the 25-year old son of a famous father, John Heddle Nash, who had given up a career as an aircraft designer to become a professional singer. One of the performances was seen by John Christie of Glyndebourne, talent-spotting as usual and following his erstwhile repetiteur's progress.

The School maintained its reputation for enterprising innovation when in December 1953, Hélène Tasartey's French Conversation Class and a section of the orchestra, chorus and dancers gave a complete performance in French of Alphonse Daudet's *L'Arlésienne* with Bizet's incidental music. The girls danced the Farandole, according to *Musical Opinion*, 'with quite a disarming *joie de vivre*' and 'the Principal conducted with exemplary tact'. Of the School orchestra's 'finely dramatic performance' in 1953 of Mahler's 5th Symphony under Norman del Mar (then on the staff) the music critic of *The Times* said 'It is a splendid reflection on the vitality of this School that it is able to raise so many players who can meet the immense technical demands that this symphony makes on all departments of the orchestra'.

Members of the orchestra were able musically to unbend (though had to keep more than usually alert physically) when in the summer of 1953 they played Handel's *Water Music* on a decorated barge in the Royal River Pageant devised by A. P. Herbert and organised for the Queen by the Lord Mayor of London. Unlikely to have been of their number, but doubtless watching them from the Embankment was a pianist who had come from Johannesburg to study at the School, Harry Rabinowitz, who became permanent conductor of the BBC Revue Orchestra. Operating in the same world of popular music was Benjamin Frankel who at this time returned to the Guildhall School, where he had once taken part-time piano lessons from Orlando Morgan, to hold master classes in composition. Besides being an ace night club jazz violinist and arranger of music for Cochran revues and Coward musicals, and one of Britain's most versatile film music composers, Benjamin Frankel also wrote eight symphonies, a number of string quartets and concertos, and an opera called *Marching Song*.

Falstaff was followed by other non-Mozart operas, all produced by Sumner Austin with Edric Cundell as musical director—*Die Fledermaus* (with John Heddle Nash as Dr Falke), *The Beggars Opera* and *The Barber of Seville*. Playing Rosina in the latter in 1954

110

was the mezzo-soprano Joyce Blackham who came from Rotherham to study opera singing at the Guildhall School under Joseph Hislop in 1953. She was heard at an audition by Gigli, and in 1955 at the age of 21 joined Sadlers Wells, having just married fellow-student Peter Glossop. The two of them were soon launched on operatic careers as top rank performers which in 1980 were still in full flood.

In charge of decor for the School's productions at this time was Guy Sheppard who was its Professor of Stage Design from 1945 to 1955. While teaching at the Guildhall School he did much of the decor for Bristol Old Vic productions, keeping links with the professional world.

Guy Sheppard designed the scenery for the School's 1955 opera which marked a return to Mozart, *Così Fan Tutte*, as usual produced by Osmond Raphael. 'Mr Cundell has trained his orchestra to the professional standard we expect but are not always favoured with at the end of a conservatory's year' ran one notice. Joyce Blackham who played Dorabella 'stood out for the sensuous quality of her voice, her musicianship and her assurance as an actress as well as her delightful stage presence'.

A royal occasion was the School orchestra playing at the Mansion House at the Welcome Home party given by the Lord Mayor of London to Princess Margaret, the Queen's sister, after an overseas tour. In contrast was the staging in July, 1955 of the musical play *Jo* written and composed by the brothers Ozah and Stanley Segal who had adapted Louisa M. Alcott's novel *Little Women*. 'Not since the day when Ivor Novello enchanted us with one romantic musical after another' raved *The Stage*, 'has anyone given us so many lilting melodies that keep an audience swaying in their seats.' But the hoped-for West End production eluded them. The Segal brothers came from Glasgow and, as they had no grant, they earned the money for their fees by making bead necklaces and marshmallow snowballs.

Also from Glasgow was tenor William McAlpine. Before winning a scholarship at the Guildhall School he was a bricklayer who had come to wartime London with a repair squad to clear up the rubble after the Blitz. A woman overheard him singing on a bombed site and secured him an audition. While at the School he had to scrub floors and wash dishes to buy himself food. In 1955 he became principal tenor at Sadlers Wells and a guest performer at Covent Garden. In

1956 he took the lead in *Idomeneo* at Glyndebourne. Still very active in the profession, he joined the singing teaching staff in 1973.

In a year when so many former students were entering on careers of promise, a guest at the annual Music Committee Luncheon in October 1955 was one who, at 76, was some way through his, Sir Robert Mayer. The more he had preached the gospel of music making, he said in a witty speech, the less he had played himself—'so perhaps it is as well to keep it dark that I was once a pupil of the Guildhall School.'

In 1955 came the first positive results of the previous year's Television Act which implemented the Government's conclusion 'that in the expanding field of television provision should be made to permit some element of competition'. It was the beginning of 'Commercial Television' financed by advertising and in competition with the BBC. It meant more employment possibilities for drama and music students of the Guildhall School. Two who immediately benefited were actress and singer Maureen Beck who came to the School in 1951, and Sally Bazely who made a great name for herself as singer and dancer in television shows, pantomimes and musicals of all kinds. Television was to do wonders for eleven-year old Dudley Moore of Dagenham who won a junior exhibition at the Guildhall School, and in 1954 went to Magdalen, Oxford, as an organ scholar. 'Steam Radio' still provided employment for past drama student James Dale (who made his debut at Drury Lane in 1908) as the name part in the BBC's long-running *Mrs Dale's Diary*.

The annual showpiece of the opera students of 1956 was the first performance of an unfinished work by Mozart, adapted by John Coombs as *Lo Sposo Deluso*, with 23-year old Barbara Rendell, the daughter of a London bus driver, who had once been 'Miss Oxford', in the lead. It was done as a curtain raiser to Stanford's *The Critic*. Princess Alexandra attended the performance in the School theatre. After playing his own score night after night (and twice on matinée days) for 18 months in *Salad Days* at the Vaudeville Theatre, in November 1957 Julian Slade came to the Guildhall School twice a week 'to play someone else's music for a change.'

It was still the mixture as before, and as lively and active as ever. 'On entering the School', Sumner Austin, the former opera singer, who had been producing opera there for eight years, told the guests at the Music Committee Luncheon of 1956, 'one is deafened by the

tutoring'. More and more group work—including movement and mime—came into the drama syllabus, instead of 'ballet' and 'tap'.

Within a few months of Eric Capon's arrival Kenneth Cork and the Music Committee chose their first Director of Music Studies: Allen Percival. Also, like Thorne and Capon, a Cambridge man, he had been teaching, playing and conducting in Cambridge for 10 years at Homerton College, with the University Musical Society (CUMS) after Boris Ord, and with the Cambridgeshire Opera Group. He had also been a theatre pit pianist in his youth in Yorkshire (shades of Landon Ronald), a professional continuo player with London orchestras and Music Officer of the British Council in France. He was 36.

Gordon Thorne gave both his Directors a free hand and both seized the opportunity. To Allen Percival, coming from Cambridge, the 'courses' for full-time students seemed, to say the least, haphazard. The would-be performer had excellent lessons with a principal study teacher as regularly as the teacher's professional commitments allowed—with the aim of 12 lessons some time during the 12-week term. Then the Registrar might 'recommend' a second study or 'suggest' a history lecture and give a student an introduction to the conductor of the orchestras, the opera producer or a 'specialist' teacher such as Walther Gruner or Celia Bizony. The Registrar, John Isard, was not a qualified musician but he had an uncanny knowledge of the professors and the needs of students, and was able—and, above all, willing—to help the new Director enormously.

There were no compulsory examinations for 'performers' who could choose when, if ever, they took a diploma. (One with a reputation for 'stroppiness'—his own word—who never bothered to take a diploma was James Galway, now probably the best known flautist in the world.) The Examinations Administrator, Leslie Fletcher, soon found annual examinations for everyone was the rule.

The lack of performing examinations within the School was strange in view of the growing 'local examinations' system. The Examinations Department was by now a separate part of the School; it administered as many as 140 centres and examinations were held at least twice a year in each centre, with specialists in each subject setting forth from London 'on tour'. The School produced its own Anthology of prose, verse and play scenes for the examinations (chosen by the senior drama professors who then included John Holgate, Rex Walters,

Rowland Hill and the effervescent Rona Laurie). Composers inside and outside the School were commissioned to write new music for the grades, which the School published under its own imprint. In December 1962 there began a series of informal meetings in various parts of the British Isles where local teachers could meet the new Directors of Studies and two examiners to discuss mutual problems and interests. From these meetings, Allen Percival especially gained considerable knowledge of the 'grass roots' from which future students would spring, meeting many ex-students now very successful in private teaching practice. Links with past students had never proved easy to forge and without the great efforts of Max Morgan (who kept in touch with many almost single-handed through running the Past Students Association with Sybil Thorndike and later Geraint Evans as President) there would be little 'feedback' on many careers.

The Graduate Diploma Course was generally considered to be for intending teachers (though by no means all graduates became teachers) and Gordon Thorne had strengthened the staff with ex-university lecturers who preferred working freelance to the haven of college courts. Together with senior staff, Allen Percival began to shape the course so that it could present an academic challenge to students as well as develop their performing potential to the full, so giving academically-minded students a practical alternative to going to university (where, in those days, little note was taken of performing ability in most music degrees). In addition to the 'backbone' of teachers such as Barclay Wilson, Percy Judd, Guy Eldridge and Leslie Murchie, he called particularly on Harold Dexter, Brian Trowell and Peter Wishart: in 1980, the first was still Head of the much enlarged Graduate Department, the second King Edward Professor of Music in the University of London King's College, and the third Professor of Music in the University of Reading.

Audition procedures for both courses in 1965 were 'informal'. Whoever happened to present themselves for audition on Mondays between January and March were given a place if, in the opinion of the Principal and a couple of colleagues, they demonstrated enough talent. Four more trombonists might be admitted on the strength of their excellence irrespective of the fact that the School orchestras had a full complement of trombones and a waiting list of seven. Percival pointed out that they must in audition try to give the School a degree of musical balance, considering the numbers of each instrument or voice being taught in relation to the composition of orchestras and choirs; and, above all, the possibilities of getting employment as a performer or teacher of an instrument of which there were already far too many exponents. He urged that the teaching staff should be enlarged and student entry reduced.

Predictably accused by some as a 'mere' academic, of not knowing what performers really needed, Allen Percival, who had been a professional musician since he was 17, persisted with his reforms; and at the same time Eric Capon changed the system which provided for the performance of only one major play a year, a few 'scenes from', and a revue at Christmas. He built up an Acting Course involving at least one full-length play a term, and made all students learn the basic techniques of singing and dancing. Capon was keen on the Musical Theatre, and under his regime would-be 'straight' actors and actresses had for the first time to take part in musicals—not operettas or light operas, or 'doing a turn' in a mock Music Hall.

Allen Percival and Eric Capon tried to integrate the two sides of the School, but found it very difficult. Musicians and actors were different animals. Theatre people were gregarious, while musicians kept themselves to themselves. Though it seemed to many a happy state of affairs to have both under one roof, each group gaining from the other, this was not the experience of the two departmental directors of the sixties—not that there was any antagonism, just little mixing. This was nothing new. It was the experience of Sumner Austin in the fifties (see page 113).

For his part Gordon Thorne was anxious to ensure that students for whom it was often a struggle to pay the fees got their money's worth. He was determined to minimise the risk that any of them would be taught by a 'professor' who was too tired or too old to give them his full attention. He considered each teacher had a mental and physical capacity, and in the interests of Student Protection the Principal limited the number of hours each should spend on teaching in the course of one day. In this the Music Committee, with whom he had established an excellent relationship, supported him. Restricting the amount of teaching meant reducing a teacher's fees, and predictably the ruling was unpopular with everyone but the students. Thorne also imposed a retirement age. Any professor who reached 70 was compelled to stop teaching; and might suddenly find himself without a source of income apart from the Old Age Pension, unless he could still derive income from private teaching or other sources. (The most resourceful of the latter must have been the pianist Enid Lewis who with her partner ran a farm breeding champion Welsh cobs.) Both the reforms, however, were short-lived. Nevertheless, the Professors' Pension Scheme which the Principal had established with Corporation contributions gave younger professors at the time the opportunity, which had never previously been accepted, to provide for the future.

Activity at John Carpenter Street was of course very much more than the giving and taking of lessons. To the Students' lunchtime concerts which still took place fortnightly were added afternoon chamber concerts. One of these concerts was given each term by the Allegri Quartet who had been appointed as Resident Quartet. Three of its distinguished members, Eli Goren, Patrick Ireland and William Pleeth remained professors into the 1970s. Pleeth in particular, the teacher of Jacqueline du Pré, played a great part in enhancing the School's reputation for string teaching.

Apart from rationalisation of the current teaching system, Gordon Thorne applied himself to the problems of the future—which meant 'the move'. To his predecessor's brief for the new school in the Barbican he added his idea of what was needed, that it should take the form of an Oxbridge college with residential quarters round a quadrangle, a communal dining hall and a Principal's Lodge. He made a tour with the Secretary of similar institutions in the United States, armed by the Directors of Music and Drama Studies with a document called 'The 100 Best Questions'. But he was already a sick man, and was unable fully to carry out so demanding a mission. He returned to Britain to resume his duties, but in April 1965 he finally succumbed to the cancer which he had been bravely disguising from his colleagues for so long. The Music Committee, staff and students had reason greatly to mourn his tragic death at so early an age—he was 53—and after so brief a time as Principal.

Neither Eric Capon nor Allen Percival was officially or unofficially deputy principal, and neither had any particular wish to become the Principal. But many on the teaching staff pressed Allen Percival to apply, with the result that he did so, and was formally interviewed by the Music Committee along with a number of outsiders. His name was finally put forward to the Court of Common Council along with one other. He told the Chairman that since they already knew him, and he had served them and the School for three years as Director of Music Studies, he was unwilling to submit himself to the procedure whereby the Corporation chose a new Town Clerk, Chamberlain or City Architect who were required to present their qualifications in a formal speech dressed in a morning suit. If they wanted to accept their Music Committee's recommendation that he was suited for the post, they could appoint him without further ado; if they insisted on his appearing before them in the traditional way, he would withdraw his candidature. The Committee Clerk told the candidate he thought Common Councilmen might regard his unprecedented stand against time-honoured procedure as presumptuous and arrogant; but in the event the City Fathers saw the logic of it and made precedent by directly appointing the man whose performance over the previous three years told more than words.

When Allen Percival took up his duties as Principal in December 1965, he remained Director of Music Studies, and made Eric Capon his official Deputy Principal. After 12 months he appointed 26-year old Leonard Pearcey his Music Administrative Assistant (later Director of Music), but remained all the while in charge of studies. Pearcey was a Cambridge graduate who had had business training, and was General Manager of the New Opera Company. He was already widely known to television and radio audiences as singer, critic, arts reporter, compere and interviewer. Eric Day remained as Secretary of the School in charge of domestic and financial administration but the Lady Superintendent (then Mary Crone) lost her Victorian title and became known as 'Warden'. In his years as Director of Music Studies, Percival had seen how little help was available to students seeking accommodation in London when they arrived, and how little information on Appointments or how to apply for work when they were ready to leave. Mary Crone efficiently set about building a list of lodgings (which she or the newly-arrived Nurse visited regularly), and began to operate an Appointments Bureau; she also gave guidance on Trust applications to needy students and arranged medical appointments at the City University Medical Centre, with which she had established a relationship. Student welfare was uppermost in the Principal's mind and the Students' Union was encouraged to play its part in improving students' conditions—even to setting up their own bar in a corner of the School canteen, a step to which the Music Committee (by then under the dynamic chairmanship of Ronald Simon) agreed with some trepidation, and which some professors viewed with horror.

Outside the School the Principal began to make his views on musical education known. In selecting potential musicians for the School, he told the Incorporated Society of Musicians, he and his colleagues laid emphasis on good sight-reading, a good ear and some knowledge of the repertory for the particular voice or instrument—'it is astonishing how many applicants, in these days of instant availability on radio and records, know so little music'—

> We look for personality, particularly in singers who generally are older than other applicants. Those who sing well but have not the personality to put it across will not make their way in the profession. And sometimes we have to say to a candidate 'Can you sing without your glasses?' But if a young singer comes along who has taken the trouble to learn some Italian, we prick up our ears. We realise he knows what he is about. Without good sight-reading a singer has not the flexibility to take the unexpected assignment. A singer must be able to do a commercial jingle on Tuesday, intimate opera on Wednesday, and 'Sea-Drift' on Thursday.

Unless a pianist was of international festival standard, he could not be trained as a soloist, but he might make an accompanist or repetiteur. Candidates with orchestral instruments should remember that the future of large orchestras was in great crisis; there was more hope in small orchestras.

In a letter to *The Times* on 'O' and 'A' level music Harold Dexter, by then the School's Head of General Musicianship, said there was disquiet among professional musicians about inadequate instrumental technique. The need was for practical musicianship; the study of harmony and counterpoint could come later. The impression he got from many syllabuses was of an attempt to produce a subject which the non-musician could study without being found out. He doubted if GCE Music could ever be a qualifying exam for a musical career; but given a radical reformation, it could become a useful part of a general cultural education.

Allen Percival agreed. He told *The Times* music critic (18 March 1966) that composers could only emerge from a study of practical musicianship. He would never name composition a major study at the Guildhall School. He told the first Gulbenkian Enquiry into Training Musicians that all conservatories should reduce their total number of full-time music students. In 1966 the Guildhall School had 500 full-time and 800 part-time students. In four years' time, when they hoped to be moving to the Barbican, he planned to have only 185 full-time music students but 2,000 part-timers.

Move to the Barbican in 1970? That was how it looked in 1966.

The Marriage of Figaro 1946

Sean O'Casey, *The Plough and the Stars*, 1969

Allen Percival
The seventh Principal of the Guildhall School
1965–1978

7 To The Barbican With Allen Percival

First talk of an Educational Arts Centre came with the appointment in 1965 of another Barbican Committee under the chairmanship of Alderman Sir Gilbert Inglefield. Studies on the feasibility and purpose of having a public theatre and a public concert hall as part of the amenities for the residents who were going to inhabit the bombed site—now grown to 63 acres—had been going on for years, but were in the melting pot again. With the establishment of Sir Gilbert's committee the residential project came to life and within a few years construction of the blocks containing 2,000 flats and maisonettes to house 6,000 people was well under way. With the installation of a new Principal at John Carpenter Street with definite ideas on the part to be played by the Guildhall School, the concept of a three-pronged Educational Arts Centre grew apace. The pacemakers were three men of a similar age—Allen Percival; Ernest Fleischmann, General Manager of the London Symphony Orchestra; and Peter Hall, Director of the Royal Shakespeare Company. At the centre of their thinking was a Conservatoire which, alone of all the music and drama schools of the world, would have a professional orchestra and a professional theatre company *as part of it*. They outlined their ideas, on which they all felt very strongly, in a manifesto to the London Corporation which lent new impetus to Sir Gilbert's plans for an Arts Centre.

In his piece 'Training Musicians for the 1980s' already referred to, the music critic of *The Times* deplored the absence of the desirable close link found abroad between student professional and his future potential colleagues. In Britain it was no part of the training of student opera singers to watch operatic productions being built up from the earliest stages of coaching to the final dress rehearsal. String players too often trained to prepare themselves for a soloist's career in which most would never flourish.

For Allen Percival the career of an orchestral player was not a mark of mediocrity. He was jubilant at the prospect of the School being connected with the London Symphony Orchestra and the Royal Shakespeare Company. Such an arrangement would keep the exacting but vastly worthwhile realities of professional life in theatre or concert hall constantly before students' eyes. 'I don't want the Barbican School to be simply a school for virtuoso and prima donna' he said. 'It has got to be a hard, completely practical training ground for the craft of music. There will be some exceptionally talented students who will go on to train for a soloist's career; but the School's aim will be to send out at the end of each year a substantial number of orchestral musicians who are prepared and fitted to make a long, useful and satisfying contribution to the musical profession.'

The plan was for students intent on an orchestral career to be attached to members of the London Symphony Orchestra as observers or apprentices. Singers would join the LSO chorus (which was originally formed by Guildhall students under the conductor of the School's Chamber Choir, John Alldis). Musical art was non-existent until the craft of music had been mastered. Singers must be prepared to spend some time in the chorus. He envisaged all keyboard players working with singers to encourage those with gifts for coaching or accompanying. He wanted all instrumentalists to study chamber music as a broadening of the musical mind and as an aspect of professional musicianship, 'not merely a glorious sociable pastime for musical persons'.

Allen Percival rejected the idea of the tower block and the Oxbridge college concept of Gordon Thorne; and the Music Committee, who were to be responsible for the design of the new school, asked the Architect Peter Chamberlin to forget all former briefs and start again. The Principal's main objection, however, was to his predecessor's belief that the Guildhall School students, the players in the professional orchestra and the members of the professional theatre company, should share the single concert hall and the single theatre. He agreed wholeheartedly with Sir Gilbert Inglefield that the Arts Centre should have its own public theatre and public concert hall, the homes of the Royal Shakespeare Company and the London Symphony Orchestra respectively; and the design of the new Guildhall School of Music and Drama should incorporate a separate studio theatre and music rehearsal hall for the exclusive use of its students and staff. This was accepted.

Unfortunately the three-man think-tank who formulated the integrated Educational Arts Centre scheme broke up within a short time of presenting their manifesto, and could not 'progress' it. Ernest Fleischmann resigned from the LSO and Peter Hall left the RSC to go to the National Theatre. None of the planners who came after ever achieved quite the same rapport. Allen Percival alone remained, and he was unable to coax any of them into pursuing actively the ideals of 1965. He soon saw the crisp vision of those days getting out of focus, and finally fading, perhaps never to be recaptured. But Peter Chamberlin was certainly inspired, and came up with the magnificent design idea of a series of studios insulated the one from the other in a honeycomb structure, incorporating a studio theatre and a rehearsal hall, divided by a central 'foyer'.

The Barbican Arts Centre was the subject of an article in the first issue in 1968 of the *GSM & D Magazine* edited by Leonard Pearcey, which became a lively forum for the airing of a wide variety of views on all aspects of the School's life. There was an interview with ex-student Barbara Jefford. In the second issue in 1969, Sir Bernard Miles of the City's Mermaid Theatre asked Why must the show go on? and quoted letters he had received from aspiring actors and actresses who were able to sell themselves confidently on paper, but at the interview 'proved to be devoid of the charm, imagination and technical skill which alone makes confidence tolerable'. John Teague, President of the Students Union, appealed to students to use their brains and not their voices by declining to inconvenience the public by demonstrating against grants they considered too low. Students were still a junior part of society, and their education was paid for by society. 'I feel that there is a moral obligation to use the aid and money given for the purposes for which it was given.' Demos might destroy the privileges and amenities they already had.

Barry Guy, Chairman of the Student Contemporary Music Society, claimed the majority of musicians divorced themselves from a large and important part of their own culture. 'Surely this is an acutely sad state of affairs—music is still music, whether stated in a Mozartian manner or in the aphoristic brevity of the serialists; surely the musician himself and the craftsman cannot ignore this? It seems he can and has—this is the tragedy .... The present state of music is diverse to say the least; but some areas of contemporary music have retained the ideas that were set many centuries ago, and although aurally dissimilar the spirit is prevalent.'

The Student Contemporary Music Society was the cradle of many distinguished performers and composers such as Barry Guy. Its presiding genius, then as now, was Alfred Nieman, himself a composer and unique teacher, who had baffled or enlightened generations of students with the mysteries of Webern and Stockhausen almost before anyone had heard their music in this country. Without him, it is doubtful if any Guildhall student in the 1960s would have left even knowing the music of Stravinsky.

In 1968 death dealt the School another serious blow: Eric Capon entered hospital for a minor operation and died of a major heart attack. The Principal had to learn, with the great help of senior drama professors like Leigh Howard and Rowland Hill, what his loyal colleague and friend had built into the daily life of the Director of Drama. In the previous year he had appointed, for the first time in the School's history, 'Heads of Departments': they were not full-time, but professors who agreed to try to coordinate the work of their departments as *primus inter pares.* They included Harold Dexter (General Musicianship), Fabian Smith (Singing), Yfrah Neaman (Strings), James Gibb (Piano), Wilfred Kealey (Wind), Rowland Hill (Voice and Speech) and Andrew Rolla (Movement). During the year without a Director of Drama they all took on part of the Principal's responsibility.

The number of public musical performances by students increased dramatically towards the end of the decade. The autumn term of 1968 saw nine chamber concerts of which one was the first visit of the string orchestra under John Georgiadis (then leader of the LSO) to the City Music Society in Bishopsgate; lunchtime recitals were given weekly; there were three orchestral concerts, three plays and two one-act operas; the Student Theatre Society and the Contemporary Music Society each had a presentation and the Student Union put on a 'Spectacular'—forerunner of the Rag Week revues—for charity, with the Prime Minister Mr Harold Wilson as their chief guest. (An alderman greeting the Prime Minister with 'How nice to see you in the City' received the mischievous reply, 'I come when I'm asked!') During the academic year, there were 136 performances in 36 weeks, all open free to the public.

The accommodation problem, waiting for Barbican, became even more acute and at least one brass professor was quite used to teaching in a disused toilet (his predecessor in the Aldermanbury warehouse at least had the coalhole). When the City of London School for Girls, which occupied the other section of the island site on Victoria Embankment, went to their new quarters in the Barbican in 1969, the GSMD took over most of the premises and there was room to breathe again. For the first time, the Drama Department had room to move in the former Girls' School Hall and its large classrooms. Ironically, the number of rooms now available in the *two* schools was more than could be planned for Barbican and when the move eventually came the new Barbican School felt (and was) smaller by comparison.

In April 1969, Peter Bucknell succeeded Eric Capon as Director of Drama. A graduate of the Royal College of Art, where he was the first holder of a diploma in Theatre Design, he had worked professionally in the theatre as designer and director and was then Principal of the Wimbledon School of Art. During his years at Wimbledon, he had built up a nationally famous Department of Theatre Design, working closely with the Central School of Speech and Drama, and he was passionately interested in the training of actors. His first task was to organise the Drama Department for the temporary move into the Girls' School. Planning the move physically turned out, sadly, to be Eric Day's last task as Secretary of the School for he had to retire shortly afterwards through ill-health. He was the last to hold the post with that title. His work was shared by the Bursar (Charles Wright), the Registrar and the Warden ... and the Principal.

'The successful candidate will need good planning sense and have some experience of budgeting' wrote Allen Percival in his specification of the job of Director of Music who was needed in April 1970 to take over from Leonard Pearcey who left to pursue his numerous freelance activities. 'Above all, he must understand what it means to try to become a professional musician and be sympathetic to the role of an administrator, as a servant rather than a master in relation to the artist.' He would be responsible for the administrative preparation of all the musical events inside and outside the School, handle Public Relations, organise entrance auditions for full-time courses and give tutorial advice throughout a student's life in the School. The successful candidate was Dr Malcolm Troup, pianist of international repute, who was born in Canada and had been a piano

131

student of Sidney Harrison at the Guildhall School in 1950.

With the move to the Barbican apparently imminent, the Corporation's Public Relations Consultant advised a Press visit to John Carpenter Street for a tour of the old buildings and an opportunity to watch the School at work.

They saw many developments of the Percival regime. Vilem Tausky, Head of Opera, was taking a class. He had come to the School in 1966 after a career with major opera companies from his native Czechoslovakia to the Carl Rosa and Covent Garden, and was familiar to millions of radio listeners as conductor of the BBC Concert Orchestra; he was also renowned (more shades of Landon Ronald) for his Sunday Concerts of Viennese Music with all the major orchestras at the Royal Albert Hall. Next they moved on to the Music Therapy Course: Juliette Alvin had founded the British Society for Music Therapy in 1958. The Principal, who was interested in her remarkable work particularly with handicapped children, first offered the Society a home for its meetings, then accepted Miss Alvin's imaginative plan for a joint course between the GSMD and the Society; by 1968, they had together instituted the first British Diploma in Music Therapy (LGSMT).

In the Harpsichord Room, they found Madame Bizony holding her unique class in 'Musica Antica e Nuova', a student class version of her professional group which had flourished since 1951 (and still flourished in 1980), combining Renaissance and Baroque music with contemporary works in the same programme. From her pioneer work came the development of the Early Music Department. In the old Concert Hall, Harold Dexter was preparing the Graduate Course Choir and Orchestra for a concert in Southwark Cathedral. In the former Girls' School, Ben Bennison—at that time England's rival to Marcel Marceau—was putting a Mime and Comedy Class through its silent paces, followed by a somewhat noisier class in 'Unarmed Combat'. A stage rehearsal was in full cry in the theatre. Forty-five professors were giving individual lessons. It was, the Principal insisted, a normal School day.

'The School in 1970 stands on the brink of an exciting future' declared the Press Notice in the kit given to each visiting journalist. 'In 1972 or 1973 the School will move to its new home in the Barbican Arts Centre, which will include a theatre (to be the home of the Royal Shakespeare Company), a Concert Hall (for the London Symphony

Orchestra), a Library and an Art Gallery. London will thus have the first purpose-built School of Music and Drama in this century. By 1974 the School will have an estimated 2,000 students. It is to be hoped that it will retain its old telegraphic address, "Euphonium".' 'It's almost the only instrument that we don't teach here' commented the Principal. (The situation was soon rectified at the suggestion of Denis Wick, chief professor of trombone and principal in the LSO, who had recently started a Concert Band and Brass Ensemble in the School.)

Peter Bucknell had settled in and was gradually transforming the Drama Department into a Theatre School with courses in Stage Management and a growing Wardrobe and Design section. Starting from the academic year 1971/2 the professional Acting Course changed from a two-year period of training to three. No public performances were given during that first year but they were resumed by third-year students in September 1972, when the plan was to give nine performances a year, including a Shakespearean play, a classical play and a musical play written by students.

Members of the Student Union felt a greater effort should be made to promote co-operation between the Drama students and the Music students, and in November 1971 they produced a musical, *Virtue In Danger* by Dehn and Bernard, which brought together singers, actors and musicians. The Union also started a weekly newsletter, *Organ*, to keep members of both sides of the School informed of overall activities.

The Autumn Term of 1971—now called the Michaelmas Term— brought several lecturers to the Concert Hall. In October Hephzibah Menuhin chose as the title of her talk 'Art as an Escape from, or a Preparation for, Life', and later the same month there was a lecture announced as 'The Fountain of Eternal Youth and Music, by its 96-year-old discoverer, Sir Robert Mayer'. Dr Jonathan Miller spoke about the National Theatre, André Previn (who was also an occasional guest conductor in the School through his position as Chief Conductor of the LSO) on Music in Films, Dr Hanna Segal on Psychoanalysis and the Arts, Felix Aprahamian on the Problems of Musical Criticism. Such lectures became a regular feature of school life and were a welcome contribution to the curriculum.

A lecturer at the end of 1971 was Henry Wrong, who had been appointed Administrator of the Barbican Arts and Conference

Centre, as it had now become. The forecasts made for the Press Visit of 1970 that the School was likely to be moving to the Barbican in 1972 or 1973 proved over-optimistic. Indeed in April 1972 the whole idea of an Arts Centre was yet again in the balance. Inflation had quadrupled the £10 million estimate for the centre, and the cost of building was rising every month. In the circumstances the Court of Common Council debated whether perhaps it would be wiser to cut their losses and abandon the scheme altogether. It was only after a five-hour discussion of some intensity, and not a little heat, in which Ronald Simon put the Music Committee's case for the central role to be played by the Guildhall School with great force, that the Corporation decided by a small margin to go ahead with all projects. A large audience of RSC, LSO and GSMD in the public seats applauded the results of the vote—most irregular behaviour in the Court of Common Council.

The students and staff from John Carpenter Street were the only people *certain* of coming to the Arts Centre at that time; but with the City's Guildhall School as the sheet anchor, it was hoped that the two other principal elements would openly abandon all alternative ways of solving their problems, and pledge their futures too in the City's Grand Design, which for so long had been a shadow but had at last been given promise of substance. The appointment of Henry Wrong gave confidence that the project would be followed through. Peter Chamberlin's inventive structure for the Guildhall School was approved, and the Principal set about inviting the staff once again to answer a questionnaire which would enable the architects to equip the studios, lecture rooms, concert hall and theatre with the furniture and fittings they wanted. Allen Percival visited similar schools in Europe on his holidays, and took a three-month working 'sabbatical' to inspect music and drama colleges and faculties in the United States, Canada, Africa, Australia and the Far East. The sights were re-set for 1975 with a new Chairman, Wallis Hunt.

In the reprieved building of the 1880s thoughts were given to the potentialities of Electrophonic Music in the 1970s which the School would be better able to explore in a building of contemporary design—when it got there. Plans were made in 1973 to set up a Barbican Electronic and Computer Centre in association with the City University 'to bring part of the musical outlook of the School into alignment with its new architectural surroundings'. The 1973 issue of the School Magazine, now being edited by Malcolm Troup, was dedicated to Cybersonics, Electronic and Computer Music System—the development of the 'private' audience enjoying music at home. The technological challenge imposed on traditional musical disciplines was discussed by John Paynter of York University; Harold Dexter pleaded for technology to patch up existing ills and not derive a new set of premises. Another author looked to a total digital synthesis of sound within commercially available computers. A work called *Hornpipe* had been written for French horn player with a cybersonic console (a miniaturised analogue computer) attached to his belt which, after 'listening' to the acoustical response of the auditorium to the sound of the horn, contributed its own responses.

The Music Hall in the Barbican School was now planned as a large studio equipped for multi-purpose TV work, with moveable rostra so that conditions for drama serials and TV opera could be simulated: the ceiling was to be covered by gantries carrying recording equipment and sophisticated lighting. The control room with observation panel was at the highest level, giving access to the gantries. Later financial stringency cut the budget for equipment and in 1980 the high-roofed Hall still remained empty, with the high-level walkway entrances to be seen at control room level, blocked up. The rocketing inflation of the seventies put paid to many exciting elements in the plans and even to some essential elements.

Thinking towards Barbican, the School, though itself still on the edge of the City boundaries, was at pains to maintain the tradition of giving regular concerts in the City churches at the centre, whether it was Leonard Stehn conducting Mahler's 6th Symphony in St Giles's, Cripplegate; Harold Dexter conducting the Graduate Choir and Orchestra in Bach's Mass in B Minor in the Church of the Holy Sepulchre, Holborn Viaduct; or John Alldis conducting Choral Fantasias by Beethoven and Holst, with Malcolm Troup as soloist, in the Church of St Lawrence Jewry.

In March 1975 John Alldis also directed a massive undertaking in St Paul's Cathedral of the 'Christmas Requiem' written for the School by Patric Standford, involving the children's choir, chamber choir, Graduate chorus, speakers, soloists, dancers and a large orchestra under the Great Dome; the huge cathedral was packed to the doors.

There were still weekly contrasts in the School concert hall—one week Celia Bizony directing a concert of Sacred and Secular Music of the Middle Ages, the next Paul Ringham presenting a concert of Music for Tijuana Band. There was still the enterprise—students of the Junior Music Department performing an opera *Dream and Variations* composed by themselves in the summer of 1975.

In his first Presentation Day address in 1966, the Principal had referred to the grand design of Sir Thomas Gresham in the late 16th century, in which Gresham proposed that the City should have a university teaching the sciences of astronomy, mathematics and physics and the arts of music and rhetoric. The City University had, he said, recently come into being from a college of advanced technology and would have a scientific bias for some time to come; the Guildhall School of Music and Drama provided Gresham's 'Musick and Rhetorick'. What more natural than that the two institutes should collaborate? Over the next decade, the School provided from its professors a visiting director of music in the University and students regularly performed there. By 1976, a new course had been hammered out in the City University leading to a Bachelor of Science Degree in Music, aiming to provide, as no other English university did, an education for the many talented young people in the country with equal interests in science and music. The School was to provide the practical training at conservatory level and the university would develop the academic studies both in science and music. Malcolm Troup left to be the first in charge of the course at the University and was succeeded as Director of Music in the School by Leslie East, who, though only 25, had already been the visiting director at the University!

Patric Standford's 'Christus Requiem', St Paul's Cathedral 1975

Molière, *Tartuffe* 1974

The Corporation of London agreed to find another £21 million for the Barbican Arts and Conference Centre in 1976, making a total of £55 million. All activity at John Carpenter Street officially ended after 90 years with the close of the Spring (now the Lent) Term in April 1977. The final Term's presentations in the School theatre were the Student Theatre Society's production of *The Matchgirls*, the musical by Bill Owen and Tony Russell, in January; a double bill by drama students, Ionesco's *The Bald Prima Donna* and Coward's *Still Life* produced by Ian Judge in February and Nicholas Renton's production of Chekhov's *The Cherry Orchard* in March. On 3 March, Allen Percival and Harold Dexter conducted choirs and orchestras in Bach's *St Matthew Passion*, with Adrian Thompson as the Evangelist, in the Old Guildhall Library. In the School theatre opera students performed Offenbach's *Daphnis and Chlöe* and Thea Musgrave's *The Abbot of Drimock* directed as usual by Vilem Tausky and from 30 March to 1 April, Theatre Workshop mounted a rousing *Oh What a Lovely War!* produced by Sid Livingstone (an ex-student then with the Royal Shakespeare Company)—the last show (it was thought) in the old playhouse whose curtain had risen on such a wealth of new talent in the 79 years since that Gounod opera and *The Winter's Tale* had been given there in 1898. The final recital in the concert hall was by Elizabeth Shenton (violin), Marylyn Troth (soprano) and Margaret Stachiewicz (piano); but the very last music to be heard in the room, in which Weist Hill, Joseph Barnby, Landon Ronald, Edric Cundell, Gordon Thorne and Allen Percival had conducted and a million young hopefuls had first performed in public, was the concert given by the Junior Music Department on Saturday, 1 April. In the final session in the bar at the end of the canteen, where students and teachers could discuss in relaxed mood the probable causes of a lack in progress in mastering the tuba, more easily find words to explain a falling off of interest in Ethnomusicology or debate last Saturday's collapse by Arsenal, there was the inevitable wondering what it would be like in 'the new place', and recalling experiences in what would soon become 'the old place'.

Never again would some 40 young men and women arrive in Room 69 on the top floor, as Neville Martin did one morning in December 1975 for the first of a two-day audition for acceptance as a Graduate Student the following September. The audition procedure bore little resemblance to that of 1965. He was 18, in the sixth form at school with another year still to go, and studying for an A level in Music. He had been taking violin lessons as an extra, and his teacher had given him the required written recommendation which he had posted to John Carpenter Street with his application form and the registration fee. He had given the Guildhall School as his first choice which, other things being equal, would give him a head start over those who gave it as their second or third, and more probably than not find themselves on the Reserve List. His parents had set in motion the machinery for obtaining a means-tested grant from their local educational authority which they would need in the event of his getting in.

Filling in the missing notes of a section of the alto part in the printed score of a Bach Chorale, after the pianist in Room 69 had played the whole piece over four or five times, was far from easy, but he had learnt how to do it at school. They had given him mock aural tests of this kind for some time, and he was also prepared for having to notate the melodies which the pianist picked out with painstaking clarity. (Little did he know that the pianist was the Principal's secretary, Mary Chapman, helping out!) In the afternoon he wrote the answers to the written exam paper designed to test his general knowledge of the History of Music.

The next day he had to show them he could play, and he brought his violin. A fourth-year girl student was assigned as his accompanist. He had been rehearsing the prescribed test piece, a Viotti concerto, at home for some weeks, and he ran through this and the piece of his own choice with her in a 20-minute warming-up session in a Practice Room. Then someone came in to tell him he was next, and he walked across the Student Common Room to a Music Studio on the ground floor at the back of the building. Here he was confronted with two men and a woman who did not introduce themselves but who he learnt afterwards were Harold Dexter, Yfrah Neaman and Suzanne Rosza.

He had never had to do anything of the sort before, and looking back on it in the canteen that last week in the 'old place', he remembered it as a frightening ordeal for which however he was made to feel very much at home by the sense of calm which seemed to pervade the whole proceeding. By the time he had finished his two violin pieces without a major disaster he was almost enjoying it.

As a candidate for the Graduate Course, he then had to show

them he could play the piano as well, and demonstrated the fact by performing his own choice on the upright piano, a Debussy Prelude. They tested his knowledge of Keyboard Harmony by giving him a simple Figured Bass exercise. Finally he had to show he could sing— and sight-read to boot. Neville was a tenor and sang, unaccompanied, a short song, the words and music of which he had never seen before they were handed to him that morning. And that was it.

'Good-bye. Thanks for coming.'

He put his violin back in its case, made for the door, crossed the spacious Common Room with its huge wooden table, and walked out past the Porter's Desk into the street. There was now a two-hour wait before returning to the School to see if he was on the list of those whom the Principal wished to see that afternoon for interview. He went to stretch his legs beside the Thames along the Embankment. He felt little urge to eat or drink. If his name was not on the list he would know the tests had defeated him, and he would have to go through the procedure all over again in an effort to gain a place elsewhere. The Guildhall School held its auditions before the others; there would be time to audition for the RAM, RCM or Trinity in April, and still start next September. At two o'clock his life was going to take a left or right turn. He had less than a five-to-one chance of being accepted, more like six to one. He knew they tried to keep a balance of instruments within the School from year to year and not flood the market with too many clarinettists or oboe players. Perhaps he had passed the tests, but they already had their quota of violinists?

All who had gathered in the canteen bar for a farewell drink agreed that standing in the crowd to search for one's name on that list was something they never forgot. Neville spotted his at once, and at 3.20, the time written opposite his name, he found himself in the Principal's Room on the ground floor sitting opposite Mr Percival who had the results of the various tests. If Neville was interested in coming to the School, then the School was interested in having him, seemed to be the message. It was a brief, friendly chat which ended with an assuring 'We will be informing you officially of our decision through the post some time in January'. Relief that it was all over gave way to jubilation, and Victoria Embankment, which that lunch time had been a place of foreboding, seemed twinkling bright.

There was still the last week of school to attend, and then the Christmas holidays. Before they ended came the promised letter

141

accepting him for the Graduate Course. He got his A level in Music in June, and reported to John Carpenter Street on 20 September. For the first term he lived at home with his parents and travelled up to London from Kent by train. In these circumstances his local education authority gave him a maintenance grant and paid his annual tuition. On Fridays he had to be there by 9 am which meant getting up at half past six, but on Mondays not until 11. On Tuesdays he went to Acoustic Lectures in the City University; Thursday was a free day. One Wednesday afternoon, after he had been there a fortnight, he and half a dozen others were asked to tea in the Principal's Room, where he met not only Mr and Mrs Percival but Leslie East, the Director of Music, and the School Warden Miss Crone. They asked him whether he had any problems about accommodation or travel, and if so, could they help? Neville told Miss Crone he felt he would like to try living away from home now and nearer the School; and within days she had sent him a telephone number to ring, and in January he moved into a flat in Wandsworth.

He was no longer a nondescript schoolboy but a Music Student with a flat of his own, new friends of both sexes to share his enthusiasms, and an enlightened master whose willingness—and eagerness—to share the secrets of a lifetime sustained him in the long, physically exhausting hours of practice without which, he knew, professional competence, let alone brilliance, would for ever be beyond his reach.

Music students are not on the whole given to horse-play, which accounted for the heartiness in the final days at John Carpenter Street being only half-hearted—a certain amount of souvenir hunting and an April Fool's Day joke which was rescued from total failure by at least a dozen reporting to the Barbican at 10 am on April the First to 'register' at the new school, including one young man who had made the journey specially from Brighton.

Moving began on 7 April 1977 and took two weeks. The main organ was left behind, the tiles in the corridors, the names of TALLIS, GIBBONS, PURCELL, ARNE and STERNDALE BENNETT inscribed on the outer wall, the theatre machinery and proscenium arch, the glass panels in the studio doors, the memories of all who had passed in and out of them.

The new building with the entrance in Silk Street was not finished when staff and students assembled for the Summer Term on 2 May; the Clerk of Works and his workmen were still on the site filling in the cracks in the floor and pouring liquid tar into expansion joints in corridors which had to be cordoned off. One whole half of the School, the Drama side, was not yet usable, and some drama students had to return to John Carpenter Street and spend the whole of the Summer Term there. They also used Wood Street Police Station for rehearsals. Finishing touches were still being made to the Music Hall, so called to distinguish it from the Concert Hall being built next door as part of the Barbican Arts Centre, and to emphasise—as indicated—the all-purpose training for which it was intended. For several weeks during rehearsals for their first Barbican orchestral concert student singers and players had to put up with electricians on ladders fixing the wiring and engineers hammering away on the pipes for the heating. The first morning of complete silence was the day of the concert itself.

Each studio had its own built-in heating/cooling system (taking up considerable space) but in the cuts made by the Barbican Development Committee during the financial crisis of 1973, the humidity control system which should have gone into the system was omitted. This saved a considerable amount of money at the time but its effect in the very hot first summer in the new school caused another crisis. Teething troubles with the heating/cooling system caused some studios to soar in temperature into the 80s, whilst professors in other parts of the building brought overcoats (in midsummer) to wear against the icy blast from maverick cooling systems! Worst of all, the instruments, particularly the 45 new pianos—including Steinway grands, as this time there had been no opposition to 'buying foreign' such as had happened in 1886—were in danger of cracking up with violent changes in temperature and humidity. During the summer vacation all the new pianos were moved into the Music Hall for their protection whilst engineers struggled to cure the system: the ranks of shining new pianos were very impressive but everyone wondered whether engineers could get it right by September. A vanload of sunblinds had brought temporary relief and the weather was suitably cool when the new academic year began. The builders were still in the theatre.

To take advantage of the large empty space above the studio heating systems, the architects had designed large cupboards, intending that instruments, bags and coats could be left there during lessons. The trouble was that only six-foot tall professors could reach the cupboards (which reduced somewhat shorter professors, such as that great coach of singers and accompanists Cyril Gell, to helpless laughter), and students moving from room to room felt disinclined to carry all their belongings with them. Hundreds of small lockers had been provided but these had to be in the basement and it took time to get used to using them. To many, it seemed the building was designed for work but not for people.

The most serious complaint by students was the lack of canteen, bar and common room within the new building. Naturally, the architects were held to blame; but history exonerated them. The Barbican Development Committee had always been urged to think of the School as part of the Arts Centre and in the completed centre plans they had included an area which was to be set aside for all the 'residents' of the Arts Centre—Royal Shakespeare Company, London Symphony Orchestra and the School—as a central meeting place for the professionals and their students, with its own catering facilities and 'common room' atmosphere. The trouble in 1977 was that the School was moving in at least three years ahead of the others and the development of conference facilities in the Arts Centre meant that the 'resident' area could no longer be contemplated (particularly as the School and the Orchestra would not make use of it all the year round). Though this was an explanation, it was no help to the Principal, staff or students in solving their problem.

In the first Summer term Miss Crone and her small team of domestic helpers organised coffee and snacks twice a day in the still uncompleted foyer, and chairs and tables meant for other unfinished parts of the building were allowed to be 'stored' conveniently in the foyer where they could at least provide somewhere for students to sit between classes. By September, a 'Students Union Annexe' was opened some five minutes' walk from the School underneath the

144

Daphnis and Chlöe and to end the evening John Alldis directed the combined forces in Stravinsky's moving *Symphony of Psalms*.

In his foreword to the booklet produced for the opening, the Principal said that for the Corporation it had been an act of faith to go on despite appalling inflation of costs, and finally to move the School in at a time of the gravest financial strain on their resources.

Once it was built, the running of the School as always became the responsibility, financial and otherwise, of the Music Committee. At the opening, the Committee's Chairman Wilfrid Dewhirst had said one third of the City's annual cash income would be necessary to finance the School—£$1\frac{1}{2}$ million.

But great schools such as 'the Guildhall', continued Allen Percival,

> are communities of people, and it is due to the dedication of teachers and students throughout the years that standards of artistic life in London, in Great Britain and now all over the world—East and West—have been enhanced far beyond the aims of those members of the Court of Common Council who founded the School almost a hundred years ago. On a sabbatical trip a year or two ago, I was greeted by ex-students of all ages in many countries, all of whom spoke of the 'friendliness' of the School with great affection. The professions of music and drama depend on the ability to cooperate with fellow professionals at all levels and we now look forward to providing our new generations of students with the highest standards to uphold when they follow their most difficult—nevertheless exciting—careers.

There were some 570 men and women between the ages of 17 and 30 taking full-time music and drama courses that term, and 1,100 part-time of whom 140 were under 17. Teaching them was a staff of 210.

On the day following the official opening the Principal told the Chairman of the Music Committee that he intended to resign his office. He had, he said, done his job in seeing the new School in and he felt that the time was ripe for someone else to develop new ideas in the new surroundings; he was 52 and needed a change. Fittingly, during his last term the City University conferred on him its first Honorary Degree of Doctor of Music, and he ended his period of office by conducting the opera course in *The Marriage of Figaro* on the June 1978 tour in Cambridge, whence he had come to join the School 16 years before.

During those years the School gained a new corporate structure, a new physical home and a new sense of purpose. Allen Percival with infectious enthusiasm and good judgement maintained the School's traditionally high standards in very changed circumstances, and earned the gratitude of generations of music and drama students whose respect it was very much more difficult to earn than in the days of Sir Landon Ronald, or even Edric Cundell.

'Camping out' in the new School Foyer. June 1977

The Barbican School from the lakeside, 1977

A Director discusses production points with Drama students in the Theatre, Barbican, 1979

A student rehearses Rachmaninov's Third Piano Concerto, Barbican School Music Hall, 1977

153

John Hosier
The eighth Principal of the Guildhall School
1978–

8 Costs Inflate: John Hosier begins to Re-structure

The report 'Making Musicians', commissioned by the Gulbenkian Foundation and published in 1965, examined the education of professional musicians and advocated sweeping reforms in the provision of specialist training at the music colleges. Very few of its recommendations were taken up in the ensuing years. One of them, the amalgamation of the Royal Academy of Music, The Royal College of Music and Trinity College of Music into one new national conservatoire in custom-built accommodation totally funded by the Department of Education and Science, was obviously doomed from the start, on the grounds of cost, of historical sentiment and rivalry, and of the belief in educational independence. The report also recommended that the intake of intending performers to the music colleges should be radically reduced to ensure that only the cream of the talent was accepted and that the number going into training for the performing profession should be related to the number of likely job vacancies.

The Guildhall School under Allen Percival was already committing itself to a policy of specialist training of students as professional musicians either as performers or music teachers, and deliberately restricted its intake in various instrumental categories to ensure maximum opportunities for orchestral playing in the School, and for eventual jobs in the profession.

The 'Making Musicians' report strongly criticised the small amount of money spent on the training of musicians compared with the support given to the training of visual artists and to higher education generally. And of course, those engaged in teaching in the London colleges were paid at a much lower rate, with much less security and fewer career prospects, than in any other branch of higher education.

London was becoming the 'musical capital of the world', with five major symphony orchestras, two major opera companies and any number of chamber orchestras and semi-professional opera groups. Yet, in spite of this, Great Britain seemed to be producing few major international soloists. British orchestral players felt that they did not have the working conditions and status of their counterparts on the Continent and in the United States. Furthermore, orchestral managers complained about the inadequate orchestral training that many applicants for jobs revealed at their auditions.

In 1976 the Gulbenkian Foundation decided to commission a new report. This was published in 1978 as 'Training Musicians'. It covered all aspects of the education of a musician, from early school years onwards. As far as the music colleges were concerned, the report reiterated many of the suggestions of the earlier one, except for the amalgamation of the two London Royals and Trinity. However it urged the colleges to reduce their number of students and concentrate on training performers and instrumental teachers. Professional courses should last four years, with a structure equivalent to other higher education courses; orchestral playing should be given a higher priority within courses; residential accommodation should be found for students; and professors should be remunerated on a scale comparable with other higher education establishments.

The Committee of fourteen who prepared the report represented a cross section of performers, teachers, conservatoire heads, education administrators and academics. One of the Committee was John Hosier, who at that time was Staff Inspector for Music for the Inner London Education Authority. The ILEA, the biggest education authority in the world, had its fair share of problems with many of its schools in the turbulent inner city areas with their shifting populations. On the other hand, it had a most enlightened policy for music, spending more than any other authority on the development of instrumental and class music. The Staff Inspector was responsible for all music policy, from nursery schools to prisons.

The ILEA had many schemes to enhance the quality of its training of the school age musician, some as a direct result of the earlier Gulbenkian report. One of them was the Centre for Young Musicians which was set up as the ILEA's answer to the Junior Music Departments of the music colleges. Because of the rates of pay it was able to offer, the CYM attracted some of the best instrumentalists in

which was given for an audience made up of delegates representing nearly all the European Conservatoires, on the occasion of their biennial conference; in March 1979, Handel's *Acis & Galatea* and Rossini's *La Scala di Seta*; in June 1979, Rossini's *La Cenerentola* was given in Cambridge and London. The producers of these included Dennis Maunder, Brian Trowell and Wendy Toye. The first major production of the new Opera Course was Monteverdi's *Coronation of Poppea* directed by Tom Hawkes with specialist musical assistance from the Early Music Department. The Summer Cambridge and London opera was *Così fan tutte*, directed by Johanna Peters.

Three weeks of 'music only' rehearsal preceded every production rehearsal: Johanna Peters was insistent that no one attend production rehearsals score in hand. The standard of applicant for the Opera Course however was high. They auditioned more than 80 for the 1979/80 course for 24 places but, loth to turn so much obvious talent away, the panel ended by taking 31. The first term of the three-term course was always probationary and in that year five were dropped at that stage, leaving a manageable course of 26.

Some 15 years ago the so-called 'oratorio circuit' was the main market of employment for the newly trained singer, but in 1980 the biggest growth area was opera. A considerable amount of work was available to the singer with personality, who had managed successfully to combine the technique of singing with acting, from the managements which had grown up around the long established Royal Opera company at Covent Garden and the English National Opera company (once Sadlers Wells) at the Coliseum, Kent Opera, Welsh National Opera, Phoenix Opera, Scottish Opera, Glyndebourne Festival Opera, English Music Theatre, Opera For All, the Arts Council's latest venture Opera 80, and the rest. In addition, the D'Oyly Carte company continued to tour as it had done ever since the Guildhall School was founded.

Productions by the Opera Studies Course were mounted in co-operation with the students and teachers of the two-year Stage Management Course which, with the Associate Professional Acting Course, constituted the School's Courses in Drama. Following the resignation through ill health of Peter Bucknell as Director of Drama in 1978, no successor was immediately appointed. In 1981/2 the Royal Shakespeare Company, with which the Corporation's music and drama school hoped to have a special relationship, planned at last to be in the Arts Centre. The RSC had never had anything resembling a trainee scheme by which student actors could learn the craft by attachment to either the company at Stratford or London. Ways were being explored by John Hosier and Trevor Nunn, Artistic Director of the RSC, through which the professional theatre company could become involved in the acting school next door. The form taken by such a relationship would affect the choice of the Guildhall School's new Director of Drama who would have to be *persona grata* with those who ran the operations at the Aldwych Theatre in London and the Shakespeare Memorial Theatre in Warwickshire. In the meantime the School's acting course continued under Gillian Cadell, Head of Acting, a professional actress of great experience. In July 1980, she was appointed Director of Drama, having brought a renewed sense of purpose to the course.

The Associate Professional Acting Course lasted three years (108 weeks of instruction). In the second year, in addition to their classes in speech and voice, movement, improvisation and play production, students were taught the Alexander Technique, acting for radio and television, and techniques of the musical, and final year students were organised as a repertory company rehearsing a particular play. Students on the two-year stage management course under Richard Curtis Berry were given a thorough training in the mechanics of presenting straight and musical plays, revues and operas, including the construction and painting of scenery, lighting, sound, wardrobe, crewing. They stage managed every production in the School theatre.

It was John Hosier's intention to remove the last elements of the Speech-Voice-and-Elocution image of the School's Drama side (still heavily emphasised in Grade Examinations held in 'Speech and Drama Solo, Duo and Group Acting and Choral and Group Speaking'); and at the Principal's prompting, Gillian Cadell set about turning the course into one tailored exclusively to prepare people for the acting profession, having jettisoned the training of Drama Teachers and Elocutionists. In 1980 the School's full-time Drama side was completely re-organised under the heading 'Theatre Training Courses', of which there were two only, a Professional Acting Course and a Stage Management Course. The One-Year Post-Graduate Course in Theatre Arts was dropped. Instead of three years, the new Acting Course lasted eight terms only. The Stage

Management Course was continued much as before, still lasted for two years and was for candidates between 18 and 24 with at least five O levels.

Over 500 men and women between the ages of 18 and 40 applied to be auditioned for each Acting Course's 20 places; and they came not only from all over Britain but America, Europe, Canada and other Commonwealth countries. They did not need to have had any previous acting training or any particular educational qualifications, though if their local education authority was to pay their annual tuition fee and a maintenance grant they were more likely to do so to an applicant with O and A levels. Everyone who wrote in was given a preliminary audition—batches of 20 in the morning and 20 in the afternoon. Each applicant was then seen individually. Forty were invited to return a week later to spend two days in the School for further observation and assessment, from whom the final 20 were selected. Gillian Cadell saw to it that each course contained more men than women in order to meet the demands of the average cast, though in fact there were always more female than male applicants.

One of the pitfalls of giving drama students their first taste of a working theatre in as modern and exciting a playhouse as that at the Barbican was the let-down they were likely to experience when confronting the working conditions of the majority of not-so-new theatres in London and the provinces in which they would have to perform for most of their professional careers. At John Carpenter Street there was no alternative to the proscenium theatre; but at the Barbican the theatre could take that and a variety of other forms, as shown, and Gillian Cadell, with the co-operation of Peter Johnson Booth, the School's staff Production Manager, made a point of ringing the changes as often as possible to give students some idea of all they could expect to encounter, from the National Theatre to local Rep.

Così fan Tutte 1980

164

Stephen Sondheim, *Company* 1980

Rehearsal for the Memorial Concert to Walther Gruner, 1980. Papagena/Papageno duet from *The Magic Flute*: Patrice Rosario, Benjamin Luxon

Uppermost in the minds of all in the last weeks of their course was how soon they would land a job when it was finished. First prerequisite was securing membership of the profession's trade union which served singers as well as actors, and several obtained an Equity card by getting a job in a theatre for a few weeks in whatever capacity while still a student, and then returning to the School to finish the course. They often obtained a provisional card by setting up an entertainment in a pub or a club; or receiving a contract from a repertory or touring company after an audition, and being given one of the company's precious annual quota of only two or four cards. Equity never admitted any to full membership before they had worked at least 40 weeks outside London, or in television, or both. Students could clock up qualifying professional work by playing for the School's own Street Theatre company started by American student Ed Wiley in 1977, which soon obtained engagements at the Edinburgh Festival, in Rag Week, for the Lord Mayor's Show and in City of London Festivals.

Students who had no immediate worries about their future were those boys and girls who attended the Saturday Preliminary Drama Classes at the Barbican for children between 13 and 15, and between 16 and 18, organised by the Junior Drama Department. Promising child musicians between 8 and 17 were similarly catered for by the Junior Music Department, re-organised under Eric Hollis, which also held sessions at the Barbican every Saturday, with the central activity rehearsing for the end of term concert. Some 150 were organised into a course of 12 successive Saturdays, each lasting from 9 till 3 in the afternoon. To take the course they had to pass an entrance audition and a written exam on the rudiments of music. The six hours were spent on a 40-minute lesson on the child's principal study instrument, attending an Aural Training Class, taking part in a Junior String Class, a Symphonic Wind Band, a Wind Octet, a choir or the Junior Symphony Orchestra, and perhaps studying a second instrument. There were opportunities for becoming involved in workshops and master classes.

A few of these Saturday Juniors applied for places on the full-time 'senior' courses when they became 18. They were auditioned along with all the other candidates. Other gifted youngsters were accepted for the full-time One-Year Preliminary Course on the understanding that they would progress to either the Associate or Graduate Course.

This group for 'exceptional cases' many from overseas, numbered only about eight or nine a year. Their instruction was planned to suit their individual needs. At the other end of the scale was an Advanced Solo Studies Course for a small number of instrumentalists with virtuoso or soloistic potential between the ages of 16 and 28—about fifteen a year. The course might be of any length with a minimum of three terms, and lessons were given individually and in Master Classes concentrating on the solo repertory. Advanced Solo Studies students were eligible to take the Concert Recital Diploma, awarded on the student's ability at a special public recital, adjudicated by a panel which included eminent performers. The level of this diploma was equivalent to a European Premier Prix. Most of the students on this Advanced Solo Studies Course were violinists, taught by Yfrah Neaman. Yfrah Neaman was appointed by Gordon Thorne to replace Max Rostal, and became Allen Percival's Head of Strings in 1966. That year had seen the 21st anniversary of the Carl Flesch International Violin Competition founded by Edric Cundell and Max Rostal to honour the memory of the latter's teacher. It was held in the Wigmore Hall, with the faithful Cyril Gell manfully playing orchestral concerto parts on the piano and Yehudi Menuhin as Chairman of the Jury. Both the Principal and the new Head of Strings determined that the Competition should either be abandoned or extended into one worthy of international status. The Principal was a Director of the City Arts Trust (whose Chairman was Sir Gilbert Inglefield) and, appointing Yfrah Neaman as the Competition Director, the Trust included a new-style Competition in the City Festival of 1968 with days of preliminary auditions and finals with the London Symphony Orchestra. Since then the biennial competition has taken its place, with the vital energy and enthusiasm of its Director, beside the leading international competitions. Yehudi Menuhin, still a great friend to the School, remained Chairman of the Jury.

Encouraged by John Hosier, Neaman's string class always had a dazzling array of talent, most of it from overseas, including a significant proportion from Eastern Europe, greatly helped by the British Council. This changed just a little the normal polarity of advanced musical education for those students who normally would go to Moscow. In the Carl Flesch International Violin Competition of 1978, four out of six prize winners came from this string class, including the first prize winner, Eugene Sarbu.

The School offered other advanced courses to singers, instrumentalists, composers and conductors who had completed a three or four-year course either at the Barbican or elsewhere. In addition to the Opera Course, there were six one-year full-time advanced courses in Orchestral Training, Piano Accompaniment, Vocal Training, Early Music, Composition and Advanced Conducting. Those taking the post-graduate Orchestral Training Course spent several hours a week in concert and opera rehearsals, as well as in chamber music and contemporary music workshops. Piano accompaniment students were very carefully selected, attended classes in transposition and continuo realisation, and were given piano and harpsichord lessons, as well as lessons with Gordon Back in accompanying techniques. Accompanying students also participated in the song classes and performed under the watchful eye of experts like Robin Bowman and Paul Hamburger. The Vocal Training Course included British and French Song Classes, German Lied, Italian Arie Antiche (Madame Bizony's *forte*), and contemporary vocal techniques. The course on Early Music was taught by some of the country's leading practitioners in a field of music that had become enormously popular. Madame Bizony had already stimulated an interest in Early Music in the School and the School now felt the need for a course to encourage those who wished to specialise professionally in its performance. With the help of the Radcliffe Trust, an Early Music Department began a three-year trial in 1969. By 1980, an expert team that included Nigel North, Philip Pickett and David Roblou ran workshop classes on medieval, renaissance and baroque music; and the students included lutenists and viol players as well as the more exotic crumhorns, shawms, cornetts and sackbutts.

Candidates for the Composition Course had to submit scores of recent composition, and demonstrate imaginative and creative flair and temperament as well as solid compositional technique. Classes included all aspects of composition including television and film, and the composers were expected to be active in promoting their music (and other new music) though the School Contemporary Music Society. One novel aspect of the course in 1980 was the improvisation sessions under Alfred Nieman. Mr Nieman was still associated with the School after thirty-three years, and always kept a fresh open mind about the latest in contemporary music. He undertook his role of agent provocateur with great relish, demolishing the routine and academic. With him in the composition department were composers Buxton Orr, Patric Standford, Robert Saxton, Carey Blyton and Francis Shaw. The School has produced several winners of important composition prizes including, in recent years, the Royal Philharmonic Prize (thrice) and the Mendelssohn Scholarship in 1980.

Only two or three highly promising students were taken on the post graduate Advanced Conducting Course, to give them a thorough practical training before they faced professional orchestras. This course began in the days of Lawrence Leonard, in charge of the conducting class during Gordon Thorne's time as Principal. Leonard persuaded the Gulbenkian Foundation to finance an international course for young conductors; the Corporation happily inherited its success by 1968 when Moshe Atzmon had won the Mitropoulos Prize in New York and it was clear that young conductors from many countries were making the course their goal on the way to international stardom. Applicants had to show previous experience of conducting, and a wide knowledge of the repertoire by ear and on paper. Students were selected by competition after a searching series of tests, including a session with the School Symphony Orchestra. The conductors' course was by 1980 in the experienced care of Vilem Tausky and most of his students have gone on to good professional careers, many in German opera houses and one to the Cleveland Orchestra. The international Rupert Foundation Conducting prize of 1980 was won by Israel Edelson, a product of the course, and many ex-students of the course—such as Christopher Seaman (BBC Scottish Symphony Orchestra), Brian Wright (BBC Choral Society) and Christopher Fifield (Glyndebourne)—came back to work with the students in the School.

In addition to these seven post-graduate courses, the School continued to offer the one-year post-graduate course in Music Therapy, including Music for the Handicapped Child. The fee for all these courses in 1979/80 was the same. Most local education authorities were reluctant to give grants for older students, and the School's efforts to invite industry and business to sponsor post-graduate courses bore their first fruits when in January 1980 British Petroleum agreed to award four annual scholarships to cover both fees and maintenance of post-graduate students. Two of them were for students taking the Opera Studies, one for Piano and one for a stringed instrument. Commercial sponsorship for concerts and opera was commonplace, commented John Hosier, but there was little industrial support for the training of the performers of the future, and the scholarships were particularly welcome. In another gesture to the School, the Midland Bank gave welcome help to the production costs of two operas.

Numerically the largest part of the School's student population were the talented amateurs who came during the day, but mostly in the evening, for part-time study to improve their techniques, widen their horizons and enrich their leisure hours without any intention of ever using their talents to earn a living. In 1980 there were some 800 part-time students who, as in 1880, mostly worked in the City and chose the studies offered by the School as the leisure activity of their choice, but a few amateurs found their feet in this way and obtained the confidence to launch out later as professionals. Private part-time tuition was given in singing and in all the main string, woodwind and brass instruments including the classical guitar, harpsichord, euphonium, lute, sitar, timpani and percussion, orchestral and choral conducting, orchestration (including brass and military band scoring), harmony and counterpoint, and composition. All had to pass an entrance audition and preference was given to those under 35. Preserving an old tradition, part-time instruction was still given in Drama, Speech Training, Spoken English, Public Speaking and Verse Speaking, and those wishing to take private tuition in these subjects were asked to come for an interview or audition with a member of the teaching staff to discuss their particular needs. Anyone wanting to prepare for the School's Licentiate Diploma (LGSM) examination in Speech and Drama could attend a Lecture Course given by the School's teaching and examining staff every Thursday evening at the Barbican between six and eight, even though they were not enrolled for private tuition. Although the School had become entirely 'professional' in its full-time drama course, it still served a need for would-be public speakers.

Part-time students could prepare for the School's LGSM in all musical subjects on the understanding that such a diploma did not confer qualified teacher status, but did allow the holder to teach in private schools or set up in private practice. The BBC's Open University granted credit exemption to holders of the LGSM Diploma. Both part-time and external students who were trained in provincial towns by teachers approved by the Guildhall School according to the School's syllabus could take any Grade or Diploma examination at the Barbican or at local examination centres all over Britain, the Irish Republic and overseas.

All these activities, the post-graduate *and* part-time courses in music, were wrapped round the hard core of the two full-time, undergraduate Courses in Music for the general training of professional performers and teachers. But those in authority at the Barbican prided themselves on having no watertight compartments. All three, graduate/associate, post-graduate and part-time, were closely integrated and mutually beneficial. The School derived considerable momentum and strength from a flexibility which reflected the spirit of the age and demonstrated the extent to which Music Committee, Principal and staff kept with it.

Both Graduate (GGSM) and Associate (AGSM) courses were of three years' duration, though there was an optional fourth year for the latter for the student lucky enough to get a grant. The Graduate Course which alone led to a degree equivalent—the 'Licentiate' and 'Associate' qualification did not constitute a degree—inevitably continued to have a bias towards those who wanted to teach. Many an intelligent wind player bent on making a career in an orchestra chose it in preference to the Associate course: one could only comfortably blow into an oboe for one and a half hours a day, whereas a violinist could easily practise for six hours without fatigue. The flautist, oboist, and clarinettist therefore had more time to give to the academic work of the Graduate Course. On the other hand, a violinist such as Neville Martin, who had started at John Carpenter Street, with no fixed idea about his future, was now in his final year at the Barbican, and had found the all-round syllabus of the Graduate Course more fulfilling.

In 1979 he was having to prove his choice had been justified and satisfy his final examiners. He gave a 35-minute private violin recital to a panel of three in May for examination in his first study: unaccompanied Bach as the set piece and Vivaldi as his own choice; sat a three hour paper on the History of Music from the Renaissance to 1980—'Discuss the lute ayres of John Dowland', 'Indicate Haydn's increasing refinement of Sonata Design', 'Attack or defend the idea that Stravinsky's neo-classical works are parasitic on the past', 'Discuss the influence of jazz on 20th century "art" music'. Not only did this violinist have to show himself an essayist, but a teacher too.

Neville's examination in his ability to teach the violin was giving a little girl from Camden School a 20-minute lesson in front of a panel of examiners, and answering questions on his teaching methods. He also had to sit a written Violin Teaching Paper.

He took a practical exam in orchestral conducting by having to rehearse a student orchestra in front of examiners. Taking them through a movement of the Brahms Violin Concerto he had to demonstrate his control, his ability to interpret the score, to communicate with the players. He had to repeat the exercise with parts of a symphony. He had been told what the orchestra would be rehearsing three weeks before, and had made as close a study of the music as the time would allow by intensive reading of the scores and listening to the records on the record-players in the School library. From Harold Dexter's Aesthetics and Criticism classes he had learnt to make appreciations of the performances of different orchestras playing the same piece, of the same orchestras under different conductors, of ensembles of the 1930s and of the 1950s. So he felt reasonably confident when he had to sit a written exam in assessing some 30 works—spotting the composer, date and style. He had had two terms at the City University on Electronic Music and, as one of a group of four, had submitted a magnetic tape on which they had recorded an amalgam of phased-in sounds created by synthesizers and other electronic equipment, which they hoped would meet with approval. From Anthony Greening he learnt about Church Music and the study of notation known as Palaeography, and made his knowledge of it manifest in a written exam paper.

Though it was not part of the Graduate Course and he took no exam in it, Neville had volunteered to take part in the seminars organised by Mark Sutton, professor of Recording Techniques, which used the high-quality equipment in the School's Audio-Visual Department at the Barbican, run by Philip Stokes. These were designed to help music students become accustomed to the microphone and prepare them for the procedures of recording and broadcasting. In another part of the School was a mock-up Sound Broadcasting Studio also used for this training. Apart from these seminars, part of the service of the Audio-Visual Department was to supply sound recordings of recitals and concerts to any student who, for a small fee covering materials, wished to hear himself playing, or, at the request of the professor, a video-tape of, say, a cellist at work to demonstrate to a student his mistakes in bowing. Students could also obtain demonstration tapes with which to sell themselves and their work to agents and managers; embryo conductors could see how they appeared to their audiences on a black and white video-tape. Although the Music Hall was still without its intended array of equipment, from a window in the studio of the Audio-Visual Department Philip Stokes could move and zoom by remote control the closed-circuit television camera mounted on the wall of the Music Hall. There was another one in the Lecture Recital Room. The department was as much in demand by drama students for whom the mastery of broadcasting and recording techniques was equally important. The latest development was a brief course on how voices were dubbed on to film.

The Graduate Course had always been what the Department of Education and Science called 'designated', that is one for which a local education authority was compelled to give an applicant with two 'A' levels a mandatory grant. Many musicians with great playing ability however, lacked the academic interest or the time to pass general educational exams at Advanced level. Ability to play a musical instrument required more sustained, motivated work than, say, studying 'A' level English, but it was difficult to quantify academically. The problem was to find an alternative to 'A' levels which would allow talented musicians without sufficient financial resources to take Guildhall School tuition designed primarily for performers—the Associate Course—for which an applicant received a grant only at the discretion of his local authority.

After delicate negotiation by John Hosier with the Department of Education, the Associate Course from 1980 was also declared 'designated', qualifying for a mandatory grant for which completion of a full-time foundation course in Music was accepted as a substitute for two A levels. Furthermore it was designated a Four Year Course with the grant applying automatically over the full period. The new fourth year was devoted to preparing for the recital examination and to learning the techniques of teaching an instrument.

This was a great breakthrough. Moreover it came at a time when central government (Mrs Thatcher's Conservative administration), in its drive to reduce public spending, was cutting back on local government expenditure, and some county education authorities (notably Avon and Oxford) were abolishing discretionary grants altogether. When the 'best' allocation of their falling revenues was left to their discretion, many were disinclined to encourage the study of music and drama as against other 'more worthwhile' pursuits. Grants to drama students had always been discretionary and remained so. Unless Business and Industry followed BP's example and did for drama students what Britannic House had done for up-and-coming musicians, it might be that for some time those who attended the Barbican's drama school would have to have the means as well as the talent to invest.

Securing the designation of the Associate Course in Music was also well-timed from the point of view of the City Corporation. The Guildhall School of Music and Drama was not a 'municipal' educational establishment supported by the rates paid by the City's property owners; nor was it grant-aided by the central government's Department of Education as the RAM and RCM were. The £7 million for the building and the £1·3 million a year for keeping it going came from what was popularly called 'City's Cash', the ancient fund maintained by the rents paid into it from the Corporation's properties —the four City bridges across the Thames; Epping Forest, Surrey Common, Burnham Beeches; Spitalfields and Smithfield markets; the animal quarantine station at London Airport, Heathrow, and the rest. City's Cash was a finite sum. No more could be taken out of it than was put into it. It had financed the building of the new City of London School for Girls which had opened in the Barbican in 1969, and the running of it. It financed the Freeman's School at Ashtead and the City of London School for Boys which in 1973 it had planned to move from its site on Victoria Embankment and re-build on one acquired east of Blackfriars. The City Architect drew up complete plans and the contractors began to drive in their piles. But the collapse of the property market brought no bidders for the land occupied by the school of 1882, and, further discouraged by the industrial depression, the re-building scheme was temporarily abandoned. The hoped-for sale and re-development of the Boys School site was linked with that of the old Guildhall School on the other side of John Carpenter Street, and the two fell through together. The annual losses sustained by the failure to dispose of the island site between Tudor Street and Tallis Street soon after the Guildhall School evacuated it in 1977 were a further strain on City's Cash. Thereafter 'debt charges' would be levied on the new School property. The original building of

1887, the annexe of 1897 and the section used by the Girls School, which had finally helped house the Music and Drama School, were still all standing empty in 1980.

Inflation apart, the annual excess of expenditure over income in running the more elaborate school at the Barbican was very much greater than before the move—and mounting every year. The Music Committee and Principal made a priority of trying to find ways of supplementing City's Cash funds, from which no more could be extracted. The City's sense of responsibility for patronising the Arts, which a hundred years ago was virtually non-existent, was now very strong, and City Councilmen were determined that no one should accuse them of being merely fair-weather patrons who disclaimed responsibility when conditions became difficult.

The great Barbican Arts and Conference Centre, of which the Guildhall School is an integral part architecturally, is proof of the Corporation's belief in investing in the cultural life of the City. Built at a cost of well over £100,000,000, the Centre, with its concert hall, theatres, cinemas, libraries and art galleries, will provide an exciting ambience for a School of the performing arts. As shown, plans were already in hand to link the London Symphony Orchestra, the future orchestra in residence, and the Royal Shakespeare Company more closely with the School.

In 1980 the School had to face further financial problems. Under a system which had persisted for a hundred years, the Guildhall School did not 'employ' a single full-time teacher. All the 250 music and drama teachers were self-employed and paid by the hour, with an annual contract for services (introduced in 1978) guaranteeing a minimum number of teaching hours for the ensuing academic year. Because of their self-employed status the teachers had no holiday pay or security, although the Corporation was operating a pension fund on their behalf. Since 1979 the Department of Health and Social Security had demanded a contribution from the Corporation on behalf of each professor which would provide an earnings-related pension, and unemployment benefits. This structure of a self-employed teaching staff had grown up over the years, before the courses in the School had properly developed. Once upon a time an eminent violinist or singer might spare a few hours from a busy professional performing life to teach at the School. He 'professed' his art (hence 'professor'). And even today a large proportion of the teaching staff are busy performers who teach for three or four hours. On the other hand, there are many professors who have the equivalent of a full-time teaching commitment at the School and there are those heads of department who organise and coordinate full-time courses, but who do not enjoy any of the security that would be normal in any other institution in higher education.

Furthermore, the actual hourly rates offered at all the London music colleges were considerably lower than those recommended by the Burnham Committee for part-time teaching and which are paid in all other sectors of further and higher education.

The professors in all the London music colleges were taking an increasingly stronger attitude towards their pay and conditions. Unanimity between them was helped by NATFHE, the National Association for Teachers in Further and Higher Education, the union which many of them were joining.

The Royal Academy of Music, The Royal College of Music and Trinity College of Music were grant-aided by the Government through the Department of Education and Science. The Principals and governing bodies of these three colleges were all anxious that the teaching staff should move over to Burnham rates and conditions as soon as possible. With the economic situation becoming increasingly gloomy in 1979, with cut-backs in public expenditure an avowed Government policy, it seemed unlikely that a deputation from the three colleges to the Secretary of State for Education, requesting that they should be reorganised on a Burnham basis would meet with any Government approval. The cost of turning the professors into full-time or fractional full-time principal and senior lecturers, all paid salaries at the going Burnham rate, would have meant a colossal increase to the grant already paid by the Government to these colleges. The Secretary of State, much to everyone's surprise, agreed to their proposal, and from September 1980 the teachers at the Royal Academy of Music, the Royal College of Music and Trinity College of Music had the same status, security and salary as any other teacher in a college of higher education or a polytechnic.

The Guildhall School had been aware of the need to look at the possibility of improving its professors' remuneration. City's Cash was already strained to the utmost by its many commitments of which the School was a major one, so the Corporation was looking elsewhere for help in funding the school. The ILEA had no music college within its boundaries with which it had 'a special relationship', and it was sympathetic to the School. Plans were put forward by the Principal and the ILEA for ways in which the Authority and the School could collaborate. For a time it seemed certain that the ILEA would be the financial fairy godmother, but the 1979 cut-backs in public spending forced the ILEA to withdraw. The Corporation had made several approaches to the Department of Education and Science for a grant to meet the cost of a Burnham arrangement with its professors but these requests had been turned down.

However, in June 1980 the Corporation decided that the professors must be paid 'market rates' which had been determined by Burnham in force at the other Colleges. A completely new set of fees was drawn up for the Guildhall professors to be effective from September 1980. These fees were a substantial increase to the hourly rate, and if a professor undertook 22 hours teaching a week he would be earning an annual income comparable with teachers on the lectureship grades in Further and Higher Education. Built into the new Guildhall rates was the expectation that the professors would give an additional amount of time, proportional to the number of hours taught, for preparation, consultation, discussion and marking. The professors at the Guildhall School of Music and Drama would continue to be self-employed, with an annual contract for services, but the hourly rates would compare very favourably with those offered in the other London colleges.

An increase in students' fees was now the only additional source of increased income for the Guildhall School. Although the fees for music courses were higher than in any other music college in the United Kingdom, even ignoring the debt charges they still did not cover the real cost of educating the student. The fee level for designated courses had to be authorised by the Department of Education and Science, as Central Government refunded 90 per cent of the fees of approved students to the Local Education Authorities who administered the awards. On the other hand, the drama and the post-diploma courses were not designated and therefore not subject to Department of Education and Science restrictions, but the fees had to be at a level that the market could stand. Students on these courses usually sought grants from their Local Education Authorities who paid them at their discretion, with no help from Central Government. These discretionary awards were being cut right back by many

Authorities, so a significant rise in fees would be counterproductive in a stringent financial climate.

The Department of Education and Science agreed that fees for designated music courses could be put up by 29 per cent and the acting course fees were increased to a rate comparable with other drama schools. Fees to new foreign students rose by more than 100 per cent to £2,400, but they were still not as high as maintained music colleges were obliged to charge by the Government (£3,300 in 1980/1).

The 'jewel in the crown' of the City Corporation had become very expensive. The Corporation had no wish to lose all control, but wished to see the expenses shared. In 1980 it was, after all, very much more than a City of London music and drama school. The only London citizens it served were part-time amateurs who came to its 'evening classes'. Everyone else came from other parts of Britain and Ireland, and every year there were some 100 students from Eastern Europe, Japan, the United States, South America, Hong Kong, Singapore and elsewhere.

For those who took bus and tube from Henry Wood House, the hostel in Camberwell for all London music students, from digs and lodging houses and 'approved accommodation' found for them by Warden Diana Howard, financial problems were on a smaller scale but just as acute—how to pay for the London fares and rents which increased with frightening regularity at least twice a year, to buy the ever costlier food and drink, the clothes and entertainment, the insurance premiums, the gramophone records, the books, the hairdos, the petrol, the soap and cosmetics, the shoe repairs, the telephone calls, the dry cleaning, the television set rental, the HP on the flute. But cheerfulness could not fail to break in to a community of young people training to be professional dispensers of Good Cheer. That it was a happy place with good lines of communication both upwards and downwards was due to the nature of the teachers and the taught, of those in charge of policy-making and administration, and of the people whose job it was to keep the basic mechanics of school life running smoothly, such as George Burns at the Porter's Desk who made sure that every new student was given a friendly welcome and quickly reassured that there was a reason for calling the Ground Floor the Fourth—the three beneath it—and that there was no need to take the lift to Studio 410. Underpinning all activity at the Barbican was universal acceptance of the fact that people came there

179

to *work* and, in the time allotted, to receive (if worthy of them) the rewards of work. People were punctual for rehearsals because it was professional and adult—and good manners. They accepted as just the 'punishment' of suspension for being late without good cause three times in a term—a serious deterrent, if one was needed, for when a student was suspended he lost his grant and it was unlikely he would find another music school to take him on. Early on he learnt the self-discipline by which alone he would be able to perfect his art and, in the competitive world of Entertainment outside, earn his keep.

But perhaps more than from anything else, harmony stemmed, as Sir Landon Ronald who created it hoped, from the presence of the Student Union and the good sense of its President who took a sabbatical year off to carry out the full-time duties and was paid a salary out of members' subscriptions, which in turn were paid by LEAs. Pauline Yeandle, elected President in May by her fellow students for 1979/80, was a french horn player and a Bachelor of Music of Sheffield University. She saw to the duplicating of the newsletter *Play On*, to furthering the plans of the Puppet Society; she kept tabs on Upper Crust, the catering contractors for the snack counter and restaurant; she organised the Christmas Party for the 'Junior' children; and, above all, acted as the mouthpiece of the student point of view which, after briefing from her volunteer Executive Committee, she expressed to the Principal.

The City Arts Trust continued its links with the School. A feature of the 1980 Festival was the City Music Trail organised by the Guildhall School of Music and Drama in association with the Trust and different commercial companies, and taking place on a Saturday afternoon in mid-July. John Denison, recently retired from the Royal Festival Hall, had first suggested a kind of 'City music tour' for children as part of his task in organising celebrations for Queen Elizabeth's Jubilee in 1976. In three city Churches and one City Livery Hall within easy walking distance of each other, four groups of musicians and readers from the Guildhall School simultaneously presented a short concert of period music with verse and prose in an historically appropriate setting. People who looked in, say, at Ironmonger Hall in the Barbican at 12 noon heard late Elizabethan and Jacobean dance and consort music, with readings from Donne and Izaak Walton; then, eating their sandwiches as they went, they could walk to St Olave's in Hart Street where at 2 pm they would hear a selection of Renaissance and Restoration English church music with readings from Samuel Pepys. A short step to St Michael's, Cornhill, brought them 'loud consort music of the City Waits' and readings from Defoe and Gray at 3.15, and, after a stroll in the sunshine to St Andrews-by-the-Wardrobe in Blackfriars, they heard ayres for voices, lutes and viols by Dowland and readings from Shakespeare. And all for the price of £1.50. Each concert was repeated at the four times advertised, so anyone could start at any one of the four locations and progress to the other three by pavement on the route drawn on their map/ticket. The City Music Trail captured the imagination of Londoner and holidaymaker, and was well patronised from the beginning. In 1980 the City Arts Trust was joined in its sponsorship by Barclays Bank.

As part of the centenary celebrations the Music Committee proposed to launch the 'Friends of the Guildhall School' of which individuals and firms could become members, make donations and endow scholarships which would enable the School to buy musical instruments, encourage world-ranking conductors and play directors to work with the School and enable it to present more ambitious productions in the theatre—above normal budgets. A contribution to these causes would also come, it was hoped, from the proceeds of the 1981 Centenary Gala Performance at Sadlers Wells Theatre by past students, which a Committee of Friends was to organise under the chairmanship of Sir Kenneth Cork, former Chairman of the Music Committee, now Chairman of the Governors of the Royal Shakespeare Company, and a former Lord Mayor of London.

There was little pomposity at the Guildhall School, and the 'Smoking Concert' (as once it would have been called) put on by the teaching staff as part of the Student Union's annual Rag Week made sure there never would be. In a programme of skits and sketches, a smattering of 'serious' music from the Peppin twins (Miss Mary and Miss Geraldine, pillars of the Piano Department), comic songs and knock-about—a dancing panto-horse, with front and rear a respected Baroque Bassoonist and Organist maybe, was always a star turn—professors let their hair down in front of their pupils and laughed at themselves in the course of a hilarious evening which could be counted on to fill the Music Hall to overflowing. A rival show in the 1979 Rag Week, which included the traditional Pyjama Jump in the Club Bar and a Pub Crawl, was a musical written, composed, directed and performed by members of the Acting Course entitled *Mac and Beth* about gangsters in Casablanca in the 1940s. That year's Rag Week resulted in a distribution to charities, such as Cancer Research, the Queen Elizabeth Foundation for the Disabled, and Spastics, of some £800.

How professors could make fools of themselves without undermining master/pupil relations would never have been understood by Sir Landon Ronald. The School moved with the mood of the day—and with evolving musical taste—and indeed contributed to the formulation of both. It had never had to move so fast as it had done in the 1970s. In its centenary year, thanks to the impetus given by Allen Percival and the current guiding hand of John Hosier, the Guildhall School of Music and Drama was set firmly on course to produce the musicians of the new world of the last quarter of the twentieth century, capable of seizing every musical opportunity it offered. They were equipped to perform not only works from the great treasurehouse of classical music on dignified concert platforms and imposing stages, but Pop, Folk and Jazz in less glorious surroundings, even stand on a doorstep to bring tuneful greetings to Mark and Madge On Their Silver Wedding Day as a Singing Telegram Boy/Girl. The jazz and pop workshop was a popular option in the syllabus which provided professional tuition in a variety of instrumental, vocal and arranging techniques. The outlets in the School had never had greater variety. Came the end of the Summer Term and eyes turned to the Appointments notices on the board beneath the Professors Common Room—the Vacancy for the Peripatetic Instrument Tutors for the Western Education and Library Board, for the rank and file violin in the BBC Northern Ireland Orchestra, both at under £5,000 a year, for the Assistant Director of Music and Organist at Sutton Valence School (scale above Burnham), for the bass-baritone in a professional Vocal Quartet at St Mark's Regents Park. Not very much there. Perhaps there would be more appetising offers in the advertising columns of *Musical Times*, *The Stage*, *The Listener*, *The Observer* or *Classical Music*.

There followed the writing of application letters enclosing stamped addressed envelopes; the decision to go back home to Newcastle and find a first job away from the inflated prices and hurly burly of London—and then be invited back in triumph! There was the borrowing of money to record a demo tape, for the new dress in which to make the right impression at auditions, for the Hire-a-Van to move the accumulated clutter of three years from the approved accommodation to make room for the red-haired cellist who had come to look round the week before. And could he draw the dole at once—'national assistance' rather? Now the sweat of it all was over, should he ask Geraldine to marry him?

The early determination to become a performer and nothing but a performer was gradually eroded as the idea of seizing the life-line of teaching became more tempting. But surely Guildhall School students who had made a name for themselves in recent times were all performers—the likes of Teresa Cahill, Elizabeth Gale, Jill Gomez, Marilyn Hill-Smith, Benjamin Luxon, Felicity Palmer, Ian Partridge, Anthony Rolfe-Johnson, Sergio Schwartz, Adrian Thompson and Takashi Shimasu?

In February 1980 Gillian Cadell invited potential employers to the School Theatre to see drama students in their final year perform the pieces they had devised for the audition they hoped they would be asked to give in the weeks immediately following their 'coming down'. 'This is the first time we have done this at the Guildhall' she wrote in her letter of invitation, 'and we hope it will be of some use to agents and casting departments to see the whole year at work in one fell swoop!' Each of the 16 students did a solo piece of three minutes, and some included a song. After an interval in which they joined the students for a snack and glass of wine, the agents watched them do eight short duologue scenes. No one was 'signed up' at the end of it, but contact had been made—and would be maintained. It was good for morale.

The main shop window, of course, for the drama students, the would-be opera singers (who also had to get Equity cards not Musicians Union ones which were comparatively easy to obtain and not rationed), and the trainee stage managers was the end-of-term public performance, straight, musical or opera, to which these same agents and managements, plus others, were asked. Here they had the opportunity to spot the actors and actresses most likely to bring life to the stream of daily television material which would flow from the BBC and the commercial programme contractors in the years that lay ahead—with a Fourth Channel to swell the number of available jobs from 1983; to the radio programmes; to the playscripts and librettos of Live Theatre and Opera in and outside London and in English-speaking countries across the world; to fiction and documentary film scripts made for entertainment and education, for video-taped advertisements and instruction cassettes. Others had gone out from the Guildhall School and made the grade. Why not me? Among the girls and the fellows in the Passing Out Parade might be embryo television producers, as many recent alumni had become; there would be others who would find their niche in the by-ways of Show Business as a Voice Over, a quizmaster, commentator, Chat Show interviewer, municipal entertainments officer, master of ceremonies in a TV 'Game', circus clown, marionettist, touring One Man Show.

The people who needed to worry were those who had never gained entrance to Silk Street, not those who were about to make their final exit. If the selectors at the auditions had done their job and the obvious non-stayer had been weeded out after the first year, there was every reason to believe that those who emerged from the School's carefully planned courses were the cream who would have only themselves to blame—and the vagaries of managements and VAT—if their talents failed to earn them a living. They were now on their own, and they would find it a very less cosy world than the friendly enclave in the Barbican. There could be no referring back to John Roffey on how best to light the battle scene; no looking to Dorothea Alexander, Leigh Howard, Faith Brook, Peter Jeffrey or Yvonne Wells on how to deliver the trial speech. The time was past when singer or musician could lean on a 'professor'. So far life had been an Introduction. From tomorrow they would have to sing (or play) *for their supper*. Among them was Neville, who would be able to boast to his grandchildren that he was one of the few who had been at both the old and new Guildhall School, and spent his final terms in the year the School celebrated its centenary.

His moving out with the rest of his course would mean a slight change of cast, but in the years to come the scene in the foyer between theatre and music hall would remain the same, though in the summer more of it was played in the open air beside the lake from which one afternoon the water mysteriously drained to soak the Circle Line beneath—and would one day return? A young man in high-heeled boots, open shirt and flared trousers embraced the long-haired, cord-trousered girl festooned with beads who sat beside him on a bench surrounded by plastic bags of groceries, magazines, violin cases and coats; the Spanish girl with olive complexion and soft dark eyes crouched on the floor to open the case of her new guitar which she proudly displayed to her English companions and, with astonishing virtuosity, still kneeling, acceded to their request to play the Cavatina which had been the theme music of a recent film; a closely cropped, bearded young man in a white polo-neck sweater and a scarf, bearing a plastic cup of coffee in one hand and the score of *Tosca* in the other, walked to the seat beside the window to wait for his lesson with Johanna Peters; a man in an overall trundled a trolley load of heavy electronic equipment into the lift ('for instruments and disabled only') and disappeared like a *deus ex machina* in reverse; Charles Henden, Examinations Director, who had served the School for 45 years, the longest of any, hastened up the steps with his Assistant Malcolm Higgins past the walled-up passage that one day would lead to the RSC theatre and considered what effect removing the bricks would have on a future which he would never share; the lively girl who had been in Kim Grant's production of *Company* pushed through the entrance door humming Stephen Sondheim's 'Side by Side'; and the young man who was to play Hotspur in *Henry IV, Part I* sat and pondered the metre of his death scene:

> And time, that takes survey of all the world,
> Must have a stop.

Except, of course, at the Guildhall School of Music and Drama.

Postlude

Sir Gilbert Inglefield, GBE, TD

Shakespeare perhaps had the City in mind when he said that Prospero's Isle 'is full of noises, sounds and sweet airs, that give delight and hurt not'. There was certainly music around in the 15th, 16th and 17th centuries and perhaps not all of it of the highest quality. Ned Ward in his 17th century *London Spy* wrote, 'we heard a noise so dreadful and surprising that we thought the Devil was riding through the City'. What was this 'infernal outcry'? The 'City Waits' in fact, a body which was possibly the first group of professional performers in England. But if they were open to criticism there were a great many good amateur musicians around. Mr Samuel Pepys was an enthusiastic one. And soon Taverns and Inns in the City organised concerts in well equipped Music Rooms. Were these the first public concerts in England? Charles II on his return from exile imported a few foreign musicians and in 1672 the first 'Recital Hall' was inaugurated at Mr Bannister's House in Whitefriars near the Temple Gate. Thus the journey from Whitefriars via Blackfriars to the Barbican has taken over three hundred years, and it has been a difficult journey.

As he looked down the Thames from Westminster Bridge towards St Pauls, Wordsworth possibly over enthusiastically thought that 'Earth has not anything to show more fair'. But the City changed, it became an image of commerce and business rather than a place for the encouragement of the Arts and an agreeable place in which to live. Has the Barbican changed the picture? Yes, magnificently.

The bombs of the late Herr Hitler flattened vast areas. How should these be re-developed? A pleasurable site for 6,000 inhabitants and a place for the Arts? There is now certainly a pleasant habitable environment for City dwellers—but what about the Arts? That was the vital question, and it had to be decided. It was discussed in the

Court of Common Council and opposition was fierce. 'Business is our business, not entertainment', said one opponent, 'not cheap culture for a minority?' The debate lasted for hours, and as Chairman of the Barbican Committee at that time, I was nearly unconscious by the end of the session. But we won. Victory was ours: there *would* be an Arts Centre and it *would* include new premises for the dear Guildhall School of Music and Drama, whose centenary we celebrate, as well as a magnificent concert hall for the London Symphony Orchestra, a theatre for the London house of the Royal Shakespeare Company, exhibition galleries and countless amenities for its clientèle, incorporated in a superb architectural environment, impeccably designed by those distinguished architects, Chamberlin, Powell and Bon. What a triumph!

How important will it be in the world of music and drama? It will mean, surely, that the City of London has one of the greatest centres for the Arts in Europe, if not the world. It is keeping up, indeed renewing, the tradition of affection for music and drama that the English have always had, and this time with international encouragement. (Incidentally, the Arts Centre will also accommodate business and international conferences so the Arts and Business are not wholly separated.) Music in the City will flourish . . . as Thomas Morley maintained it always had, in the quotation which began Part Two of this story of the GSMD. But it was a struggle to maintain the tradition and Inglefield will never forget the battlefield of the Barbican in 1965.

Acknowledgements

Research means listening as well as reading. Here I am glad to have the opportunity to express my thanks to busy people who gave of their time to talk to me—Mr Maurice Hart, chairman of the Music Committee; Mr John Hosier, Principal; Mr Leslie East, Director of Music; Mr Alan Tait, General Administrator; Mr Charles Wright, Bursar; Mr Charles Henden, Examinations Director; Mr Paul Holden, Senior Librarian; Mr Peter Johnson Booth, Production Manager; Mr Philip Stokes, Audio Visual Technician; staff and students including Miss Gillian Cadell, Mr Neville Martin, Mr Max Morgan, Mr Peter Newham, Mr Buxton Orr, Miss Johanna Peters, Mr Arthur Reckless, Miss Pauline Yeandle; and Mr Allen Percival, past Principal.

I am also indebted to the help given me by the staff of the Guildhall Library and John Fisher of the Prints and Drawings Department, and of the Corporation of London Records Office, and Public Relations Office.

Acknowledgement is also due to the following for photographs: Guildhall Library (pp. 10, 34, 42, 43, 46, 47, 55, 56, 57, 58, 66), Photopress (pp. 74, 124), Tom L. Blau (pp. 90, 106, 107), R. Brown (pp. 125, 138), Photographia (p. 126), The Guardian (p. 137), Public Relations Office, Guildhall (pp. 150, 151, 152, 153, 154), Donald Southern (p. 164), Carole Latimer (p. 165).

H. B-K.

Music Committee for 1980/1

Chairman	Maurice George Hart
Deputy Chairman	Cyril Henry Murkin
Aldermen	Richard Christopher Larkins Charvet
	Colonel Greville Douglas Spratt
Commoners	Francis McWilliams
	Philip Henry Cresswell
	Ronald Derek Keep Edwards
	John Clarence Lascelles
	Leslie Barnett Prince, *Deputy*
	Esmond Patrick Thomson Roney
	Charles Edward Frapell
	Ivor Bowen
	Richard Saunders
	Robert Gold
	Peter Anthony Bull
	Michael Henderson-Begg
	Matthew Henry Oram
	Herbert Twyneham Pike
	Richard Arthur Austin-Cooper
	Rosemary Humphrays
	Dr Keith Gugan
	Raymond Cecil Deith
	William Harold Wylie Harris
	Ross Anthony Fitzpatrick
	June Evans
	John Steven Henderson
	Ian David McNeil
	Geoffrey Clive Henry Lawson
	Ivy Margaret Sharp
	Edward John Reed
	Peter Dudley Northall-Laurie
together with	Thomas William Fripp
	Alderman Alan Towers Traill
	Wilfrid Dewhirst, *Deputy*
	Alderman Sir Henry Murray Fox

Chronological Table

1880   April 30: Musical Deputation Report to Court of Common Council recommends establishment of a School of Music in the City; it is accepted.
September 26: GUILDHALL SCHOOL OF MUSIC opens in converted warehouse at 16 Aldermanbury with T H Weist Hill as Principal.

1882   Music Deputation changes name to 'Music Committee'.
City of London School for Boys moves to Victoria Embankment.

1883   National Training School for Music re-structured as 'Royal College of Music', and is opened by HRH The Prince of Wales in same building in Kensington.

1885   July 21: Pearse Morrison lays foundation stone of new Guildhall School of Music in John Carpenter Street off Victoria Embankment.

1886   December 9: Lord Mayor of London opens new building.

1891   December 26: T H Weist Hill dies; Sir Joseph Barnby succeeds as Principal.

1896   Sir Joseph Barnby dies; Dr W H Cummings succeeds as Principal.

1897   Foundation stone laid of extension to John Carpenter Street building.

1898   July 11: Lord Mayor opens extension (containing theatre).

1910   October 6: Dr W H Cummings retires; Landon Ronald succeeds as Principal, and introduces first official curriculum.

1914–18 Guildhall School carries on throughout World War I.

1915   June 10: Dr W H Cummings dies.

1922   Landon Ronald knighted.
Formation of British Broadcasting Company.

1930   JUBILEE OF GUILDHALL SCHOOL OF MUSIC.

1934	Henry Saxe Wyndham retires as Secretary after 33 years. Sir Landon Ronald's Silver Jubilee.
1935	The words 'and Drama' added to School's title.
1936	BBC launches world's first public television service.
1938	Sir Landon Ronald retires as Principal of Guildhall School of Music and Drama on reaching age of 65; Edric Cundell succeeds him.
1939	September 3: start of World War II; Guildhall School carries on; TV suspended.
1942	Diploma of Honorary Membership instituted.
1945	Carl Flesch Open Violin Competition launched in his memory.
1945	End of World War II; American servicemen attend School. Junior Exhibition Scheme inaugurated. BBC resume television broadcasts.
1955	First Commercial Television programmes. Corporation urge residential scheme for bombed site of the Barbican; instruct architects to draw up plan including a new Guildhall School.
1958	Edric Cundell retires as Principal on reaching age of 65, and is succeeded by Gordon Thorne.
1962	Allen Percival appointed Director of Music Studies; and Eric Capon, Director of Drama.
1965	Death of Gordon Thorne; Allen Percival succeeds as Principal; Eric Capon becomes Deputy Principal.
1966	Hopes of moving to the Barbican in 1970; plans made for an Educational Arts Centre to embrace Guildhall School, public theatre for Royal Shakespeare Company and public concert hall for London Symphony Orchestra.
1969	School takes over space vacated by City of London School for Girls.
1977	April: School completes last term at John Carpenter Street. May: School opens in new building in the Barbican. November 16: Allen Percival resigns as Principal and is succeeded by John Hosier (from June 1978).
1980	CENTENARY OF GUILDHALL SCHOOL OF MUSIC AND DRAMA.

Index

f = footnote